D1515781

# BEST HIKES OF THE
# APPALACHIAN
# TRAIL

## *New England*

### Connecticut · Massachusetts · Vermont · New Hampshire · Maine

# LAFE LOW

**MENASHA RIDGE PRESS**
Your Guide to the Outdoors Since 1982

APPALACHIAN TRAIL
CONSERVANCY®

**Best Hikes of the Appalachian Trail: New England**

Copyright © 2016 by Lafe Low
All rights reserved
Copublished by Menasha Ridge Press and Appalachian Trail Conservancy
Distributed by Publishers Group West
Printed in the United States of America
First edition, first printing

Cover design by Scott McGrew
Text design by Annie Long
Cartography and elevation profiles by Scott McGrew
Cover photos (clockwise from top): Hike 45, Katahdin; Hike 7, Jug End State
Reservation; Hike 32, Mount Moosilauke; Hike 45, Katahdin
Frontispiece: Jeffers Brook at the end of Townline Trail (see page 186)
All cover and interior photographs, unless otherwise noted, by Lafe Low
The Appalachian Trail symbol is a registered trademark of Appalachian Trail Conservancy.

Library of Congress Cataloging-in-Publication Data

Names: Low, Lafe, 1952-
Title: Best hikes of the Appalachian Trail : New England / Lafe Low.
Description: First edition. | Birmingham, AL : Menasha Ridge Press, [2016] |
   "Distributed by Publishers Group West"--T.p. verso. | Includes index.
Identifiers: LCCN 2015045322| ISBN 9780897324762 | ISBN 9780897324779
(eBook)
Subjects: LCSH: Hiking—Appalachian Trail—Guidebooks. | Hiking—Connecticut—
Guidebooks. | Hiking—Vermont—Guidebooks. | Hiking—New Hampshire—
Guidebooks. | Hiking—Maine—Guidebooks. | Appalachian Trail—Guidebooks.|
Connecticut—Guidebooks. | Vermont—Guidebooks. | New Hampshire—
Guidebooks. | Maine—Guidebooks.
Classification: LCC GV199.42.A68 .L655 2016 | DDC 796.510974--dc23
LC record available at http://lccn.loc.gov/2015045322

 **MENASHA RIDGE PRESS**
An imprint of AdventureKEEN
2204 First Ave. S., Suite 102
Birmingham, AL 35233

**APPALACHIAN TRAIL CONSERVANCY**
799 Washington St.
Harpers Ferry, WV 25425
**appalachiantrail.org**

Visit **menasharidge.com** for a complete listing of our books and for ordering
information. Contact us at our website, at **facebook.com/menasharidge,** or at
**twitter.com/menasharidge** with questions or comments. To find out more about
who we are and what we're doing, visit our blog, **trekalong.com.**

DISCLAIMER
This book is meant only as a guide to select routes along the Appalachian Trail. This
book does not guarantee hiker safety in any way—you hike at your own risk. Neither
Menasha Ridge Press nor Lafe Low is liable for property loss or damage, personal injury,
or death that result in any way from accessing or hiking the trails described in the
following pages. Please be especially cautious when walking in potentially hazardous
terrains with, for example, steep inclines or drop-offs. Do not attempt to explore
terrain that may be beyond your abilities. Please read carefully the introduction to this
book as well as further safety information from other sources. Familiarize yourself
with current weather reports and maps of the area you plan to visit (in addition to the
maps provided in this guidebook). Be cognizant of park regulations and always follow
them. Do not take chances.

# Contents

# Dedication

*This book is dedicated to my best hiking, camping, and skiing buddy—my son, Devin Low.*

# Acknowledgments

**WHILE I DID MOST OF THESE HIKES SOLO,** I did enjoy some fantastic company on several of them. I would be remiss if I did not acknowledge the family and friends I dragged along with me on some of these hikes.

Devin Low accompanied me on the spectacularly scenic Cascade Brook Trail in the White Mountains of New Hampshire.

Scott Shultz accompanied me on several hikes—Mount Algo in Connecticut, Mount Moosilauke in New Hampshire, and Mount Everett in Massachusetts. That worked out to be the first hike, one right in the middle, and the last hike.

Heather Johnson and Anthony Cantlin accompanied me up the impressively steep Holts Ledges in New Hampshire.

Peter Tamposi and Brian Merritt both joined me for the ascent of the mighty Katahdin in Baxter State Park, Maine—the northern terminus of the Appalachian Trail.

# Preface

**NEW ENGLAND IS A REMARKABLY DIVERSE** and dramatically beautiful region. As a lifelong New Englander, I've had the pleasure of traveling around the region to enjoy the mountains, the rivers, the lakes, and the oceans. The Appalachian Trail (A.T.) cuts a circuitous swath through many of the most spectacular mountains and ranges in western Connecticut, Massachusetts, Vermont, New Hampshire, and Maine. Along the way, it leads you across pastoral fields, through forests that look like something out of Winnie-the-Pooh's Hundred Acre Wood, along pristine rivers and streams, and over the dramatic mountain ridgelines of the Green Mountains, the White Mountains, and the ranges of western Maine.

I have long journeyed to the mountains to hike and camp and to just be in the woods. I have my favorite trails and my favorite areas. I knew that by researching and writing this guidebook, I would have to step out of my routine, go beyond my familiar places, and explore new hikes and mountains of which I had heard but never explored myself. And for that opportunity and privilege, I am truly thankful. I will return to these trails and mountains, as my list of favorite places now includes Old Speck, Mount Liberty, and Jug End State Reservation.

In a single day on the Appalachian Trail in New England, you can find yourself following the trail through rolling hills and fields, along raging rivers, and up and over precipitously steep mountainsides. You'll pass through open meadows and orchards, as well as forest so dense that you couldn't wander off the trail if you tried. The Appalachian Trail has it all as it traverses New England—from the short and sometimes impressively steep hills in western Connecticut, up through the increasingly high and steep mountains of Massachusetts, to the towering massifs of Vermont, New Hampshire, and ultimately Katahdin, the northern terminus of the Appalachian

**BROMLEY MOUNTAIN TRAIL OVERLAPS WITH LONG TRAIL.** *(See page 118.)*

Trail and the highest point in the state of Maine. Hiking the Appalachian Trail in New England will test you, it will amaze you, and it will reward you.

One other note of which you may or may not be aware. Appalachian Trail thru-hikers adopt trail names. Often, these are bestowed upon them by friends, family, or fellow hikers. I had the pleasure of chatting with Blacksquatch, Balderdash, and Tomfoolery on several of these hikes. While I am not yet a thru-hiker, I decided to adopt a trail name, one that would reflect the nature of this group of hikes I was undertaking, as well as my love of music, especially The Beatles. So my trail name for this summer of hiking—Day Tripper.

# Hiking Recommendations

**ALMOST ANY HIKE DESCRIBED** in this book will have at least a little scenery, wildlife, and views, and your dog and your kids will easily enjoy them. Out of the whole bunch, though, several stand out for the following attributes.

## Best for Scenery

16   Harmon Hill (p. 108)
21   White Rock Ledge (p. 133)
33   Cascade Brook Trail (p. 195)
36   Old Speck (p. 214)
43   Pleasant Pond Mountain (p. 252)

## Best for Wildlife

26   Holts Ledges (p. 160)
27   Smarts Mountain (p. 165)
34   Mount Liberty (p. 200)
44   Little and Big Niagara Falls (p. 258)

## Best for Seclusion

38   Moody Mountain (p. 225)
39   Old Blue Mountain (p. 230)
41   South Pond (p. 242)
42   West Carry Pond (p. 247)

## Best for Kids

13   Warner Hill (p. 92)
20   Little Rock Pond (p. 128)
29   Ore Hill (p. 176)
35   Rattle River Trail (p. 206)
44   Little and Big Niagara Falls (p. 258)

## Best for Dogs

## Best for Waterfalls

## Best for History

## Best for Geology

## Best for Wildflowers

**THE ROCKY MOONLIKE LANDSCAPE OF THE TABLELANDS ON THE UPPER REACHES OF KATAHDIN** *(See page 264.)*

## Best for a Workout

## Best for Views

**LOOKING OUT INTO FRANCONIA NOTCH ON CASCADE BROOK TRAIL**
*(See page 195.)*

# Introduction

**THE APPALACHIAN TRAIL WINDS** through five of the six New England states. From the short, rolling hills of western Connecticut, the trail heads mostly north through western Massachusetts and the Berkshires. Leaving Massachusetts, it travels through south-central Vermont. Here the mountains start to get a bit more serious. You'll soon see how Vermont earned its nickname: the Green Mountain State.

In the central eastern region of Vermont, you'll pass into New Hampshire—the Granite State and home to the impressively steep White Mountains. Here the Appalachian Trail traverses the Franconia Ridge and the Presidential Range, and passes up and over the summit of Mount Washington—the high point of New England and home to the highest wind gusts ever recorded. After climbing your way through New Hampshire, you'll enter western Maine near Grafton Notch State Park.

The trail through Maine is peppered with steep climbs and long stretches of backcountry. In fact, in northwestern Maine you'll encounter the 100 Mile Wilderness—the wildest and one of the most challenging sections of true backcountry on the Appalachian Trail. It starts in Monson, designated an official Appalachian Trail Community, and runs to just south of the Abol Bridge in Baxter State Park. Continuing north, you will, of course, come to Katahdin—the highest point in Maine and the northern terminus of the Appalachian Trail. This is a dramatic, sturdy climb that awaits thru-hikers finishing their south-to-north route.

The Appalachian Trail in New England will bring you through a bit of everything—relatively gentle meandering through the woods, following the shores of lakes or rivers, pastoral fields, and orchards, and then much steeper hikes up increasingly larger mountains, including areas of hand-over-hand scrambling and parts of the trail equipped with iron bars to aid your passage. This is called *via ferrata*, or the "iron way." This was something first used during World War II in the Dolomites in Italy to help troops traverse difficult alpine routes without requiring additional climbing gear.

Because the Appalachian Trail in New England will present you with a bit of everything, you should be ready for anything. The following sections will describe how to use this book, how to interpret the trail ratings, and what you should carry with you as you hike portions of this fabled footpath.

# About This Book

**THE 45 TRAIL PROFILES** for the day hikes listed in this book are organized from south to north, starting in eastern New England at the Connecticut–New York border and going all the way up to Katahdin in central Maine. It was fairly straightforward to determine how many hikes to include in each state. This book was to include 45 day hikes. Therefore, I allotted 10 each to the northern New England states of Maine, New Hampshire, and Vermont. Those states are home to some impressive mountain ranges. I also chose to pursue 10 hikes in western Massachusetts, as the Berkshires and Mount Greylock are also spectacular areas. The A.T. spends less time in the northwestern corner of Connecticut, so I did five hikes there, though those are also some spectacularly scenic hikes.

The intent here is also to present a decent mix of hikes—some good for bringing the kids on their first hike, some good for kids who have been in the woods a few times already, some a bit more challenging, and some extremely challenging for seasoned hikers looking for a true backcountry mountain experience. Use the star ratings that accompany each hike profile to help you find the right hike to best suit your mood. These will give you a snapshot of what to expect on the hike, such as how strenuous, scenic, and secluded it will be— among other things.

Some hikes are quite popular, so you're bound to have some company on the trail. Others are extremely remote, and you quite possibly won't see anyone else throughout your hike. Some hikes take you through dense forest and end on a subtle, densely forested summit plateau. Others wind past waterfalls and ravines and end with spectacular, sweeping views of the surrounding backcountry. Hikers have different priorities when they lace up their hiking boots. What's important to you might not be as important to others. Some may want the woods to themselves and others may need a panoramic vista at the end of the long climb.

Hike information boxes at the start of each profile give you what you need to know when selecting a hike, and the hike profiles themselves take you on guided tours, so you'll know what to expect and when.

## How to Use This Guidebook

THE FOLLOWING SECTIONS will walk you through each of the organizational elements of the profiles as they're presented in this book. The goal is to make it as easy as possible for you to plan a hike you'll enjoy, a hike you'll remember, and a hike that matches whatever you're looking for on any given day.

### Overview Map & Map Key

The overview map on the inside front cover shows the general location of each hike's primary trailhead. By seeing the trailheads on a regional map of New England, you can pick out the hikes that are closest to you or are located in an area to which you'll be traveling. Each hike's number appears on the overview map, on the map key facing the overview map, and in the table of contents. Thus, if you know you will be traveling to a particular area, you can check that area on the overview map, find the appropriate hike numbers, and then flip through the book and easily find those hikes by looking up the hike numbers at the top of each profile page. Or if you find a specific hike on the overview map, you can locate the profile by following the number.

## Trail Maps

Besides the overview map on the inside cover, a detailed map of the hike route accompanies each individual profile. On these maps, symbols indicate the complete route and topographic landmarks, such as creeks, overlooks, and peaks.

To produce the highly accurate maps in this book, the author used a handheld GPS unit to gather data while hiking each route, and then sent that data to the publisher's expert cartographers. However, your GPS is never a substitute for sound, sensible navigation that takes into account the conditions that you observe while hiking. The GPS is a remarkable tool, but it can't replace knowing how to use a map and compass. If you're interested in learning more about using a GPS for navigation, check out *Outdoor Navigation with GPS*, third edition, by Stephen W. Hinch. Be sure to check out books and articles, or even take a class at your local outdoor store, on using a map and compass as well.

Further, despite the high quality of the maps in this guidebook, the publisher and author strongly recommend that every time you venture out into the woods, you always carry an additional, accurate, up-to-date map of the area in which you're hiking, such as the ones noted in each entry opener's listing for "Maps."

## Elevation Profile (Diagram)

This diagram represents the rises and falls of the trail as viewed from the side over the complete distance (expressed in miles) for that trail. From this, you should be able to judge where the steep sections will come during the hike. Don't underestimate the intensity of a hike that may be associated with these diagrams. The profile for the Old Blue Mountain hike in Maine, for example, shows an intensely steep beginning. That is quite accurate.

On the diagram's vertical axis, or height scale, the number of feet indicated between each tick mark lets you visualize the climb. Use these side-view profiles, along with contour markings on the additional maps you will carry, to determine the relative intensity of the hike. To avoid making flat hikes look steep and steep hikes appear flat, varying height scales provide an accurate image of each hike's climbing challenge. For example, one hike's scale might rise to more than 4,000 feet, while others may reach only 1,000 feet.

## The Hike Profile

Each hike profile opens with an information box that encapsulates all the details you'll need to know for that particular hike. The at-a-glance information includes the hike's star ratings (for hike difficulty, how appropriate the hike is for kids, scenery, trail condition, and solitude), GPS trailhead coordinates, the overall distance of the hike, trail configuration (out-and-back or point-to-point), and contacts for local information. Each profile also includes a listing of the appropriate maps to have on hand for the hike (see "Trail Maps," page 4).

The text for each profile includes four sections: Overview, Route Details, Nearby Attractions, and Directions (for driving to the trailhead area). Below is an explanation of each of these elements.

★ **Overview** gives you a quick summary of what to expect on the trail.

★ **Route Details** takes you on a guided hike from start to finish, including landmarks, side trips, and possible alternate routes along the way.

★ **Nearby Attractions** mentions the nearest towns, as well as other trails or parks close by.

★ **Directions** will get you to the trailhead from a well-known road or highway.

### STAR RATINGS

Here's a guide to interpreting the rating system of one to five stars in each of the five categories for each hike—scenery, trail condition, children, difficulty, and solitude.

#### SCENERY:

★★★★★ Unique, picturesque panoramas

★★★★ Diverse vistas

★★★ Pleasant views

★★ Unchanging landscape

★ Unremarkable

**TRAIL CONDITION:**

★ ★ ★ ★ ★   Consistently well maintained

★ ★ ★ ★   Stable, with no surprises

★ ★ ★   Average terrain to negotiate

★ ★   Inconsistent, with good and poor areas

★   Rocky, overgrown, or often muddy

**CHILDREN:**

★ ★ ★ ★ ★   Appropriate for babes in strollers

★ ★ ★ ★   Fun for any kid past the toddler stage

★ ★ ★   Good for young hikers with proven stamina

★ ★   Not enjoyable for children

★   Not advisable at all for children

**DIFFICULTY:**

★ ★ ★ ★ ★   Grueling

★ ★ ★ ★   Strenuous

★ ★ ★   Moderate (won't beat you up—but you'll know you've been hiking)

★ ★   Easy with patches of moderate intensity

★   Good for a relaxing stroll

**SOLITUDE:**

★ ★ ★ ★ ★   Positively tranquil

★ ★ ★ ★   Spurts of isolation

★ ★ ★   Moderately secluded

★ ★   Could be crowded on weekends and holidays

★   Steady stream of individuals and/or groups

## GPS TRAILHEAD COORDINATES

Each profile provides GPS coordinates to the primary trailhead. Keep this information handy, as some of the trailheads can be a challenge to locate. Some are situated off extremely remote fire roads or logging roads. Miss the trailhead and you can easily go well out of your way.

In the opener for each hike profile, find the GPS coordinates. These represent the intersection of the latitude (north–south) and longitude (east–west) lines that pinpoint the precise trailhead location. Plug these into your own handheld GPS unit or your phone if you prefer to use that. And remember, a handheld GPS unit or GPS app in your phone does not replace having a map and compass and the knowledge to use them properly.

In some cases, you can park right at the trailhead. Other hiking routes require a short walk to the trailhead from a parking area. This information is also noted in the hike profiles.

You are most likely familiar with the latitude and longitude grid system, but here's a brief refresher that will help you visualize the GPS coordinates: Imaginary lines of latitude—called parallels and approximately 69 miles apart from each other—run horizontally around the globe. The equator is established at 0°. Each parallel is indicated by degrees, increasing from the equator: up to 90°N at the North Pole and down to 90°S at the South Pole.

Imaginary lines of longitude—called meridians—run perpendicular to latitude lines and are likewise indicated by degrees. Starting from 0° at the Prime Meridian in Greenwich, England, they continue to the east and west until they meet 180° later at the International Date Line in the Pacific Ocean. At the equator, longitude lines also are approximately 69 miles apart, but that distance narrows as the meridians converge toward the North and South Poles.

The GPS coordinates map to latitude and longitude and are generated by a network of 24 geosynchronous satellites positioned such that they cover Earth's entire surface. A GPS unit locks onto at least three or four of those satellites to triangulate position. The system works well, but reception can be stymied by weather, dense forests, or deep canyons. To convert GPS coordinates given in degrees, minutes, and seconds to the degrees–decimal minutes format, divide the seconds by 60. For more on GPS technology, visit **usgs.gov.**

## DISTANCE & CONFIGURATION

The distance is the full, round-trip length of the hike from start to finish. If the hike description includes options for a shorter or longer hike, those round-trip distances will also be described here.

The configuration defines the trail as an out-and-back (taking you in and out via the same route, such as hiking to the summit of a mountain and then down the same way), point-to-point, or some other configuration.

## HIKING TIME

In most mountainous regions like the Green Mountains of Vermont, the White Mountains of New Hampshire, and the Mahoosuc Range in western Maine, the general rule of thumb for the hiking times is 1 hour per 1 mile and 1,000 feet of elevation gain. Not all hikes even have that much elevation gain, and others are steep and rocky and would probably result in a slower pace. Check the summary information and the text of the hike profiles, which will provide as much detail as possible.

That pace also allows time for taking photos, for stopping to admire the views (of which there are many), and for alternating stretches of steep hills, rolling forest floors, and gentle descents. When you're deciding whether or not to follow a particular trail described in this guidebook, be flexible. Consider your own pace, the weather, your general physical condition, and your energy level on that day.

## HIGHLIGHTS

Many of these hikes take you past spectacular highlights, which will be noted here. These may include waterfalls, massive cliffs, or particularly scenic views from the summit.

## ELEVATION

In each hike's key information, you'll see the elevation at both the trailhead and the peak. The full hike profile also includes a complete elevation profile (see "Elevation Profile," page 4).

## ACCESS

No fees are required for any of these hikes. However, trailhead parking fees will sometimes be noted here. If there are any restrictions on hours to access the trail (such as sunrise–sunset), that will also be mentioned here.

## MAPS

Maps of your hiking route and the surrounding area are essential. A GPS unit or GPS app on your phone is a useful tool, but it's no replacement for detailed, up-to-date maps. This section will list any additional maps you could and should carry with you for the hike being profiled. Maps can be purchased from the Appalachian Trail Conservancy at **atctrailstore.org.**

## CONTACT

Listed here are websites for checking trail conditions and gleaning other day-to-day information.

# Weather

**THERE ARE MYRIAD OLD SAYINGS** about the weather in New England. "If you don't like the weather, just wait a few minutes and it will change. New England has five seasons: summer, fall, winter, spring, and mud. In northern New England, some say there are only two seasons: 10 months of winter and 2 months of poor sledding."

You get the picture. The weather in New England is variable. Be ready for anything. Expect anything. Even in the summer, have a fleece jacket and hat. You could be hot and sweaty hiking up a massif like Mount Liberty in New Hampshire, only to find chilly temperatures and howling winds at the summit.

You can hike the Appalachian Trail in all 12 months of the year; however, if there is snow or ice October 15–May 15 on Katahdin, you will need a special permit. Obviously if you're going to be hiking in the winter, you better have the right equipment and the right experience to handle the rigors of winter hiking and mountaineering.

Every season has its pros and cons—thankfully always more pros than cons. Spring can be an excellent time to hike, as it may be a bit less buggy. It can also be extraordinarily muddy in some sections, so be ready for that. Summer is obviously the prime time for hiking, but you'll need to keep an eye on the variable weather. Fall is a delightful time to hike in New England, but do be wary of the blanket of leaves that will inevitably cover the forest floor. The leaves covering the trail can make staying on the trail a challenge and can make for slick footing in the steeper sections.

To give you an idea of what you might expect throughout the year when hiking in New England, the following chart lists the average high and low temperatures and average precipitation by month for each New England state through which the Appalachian Trail passes. Note that the temperatures given here are from stations in cities and towns; for higher elevations, subtract 3.5°F per 1,000 feet of elevation from the nearest recording station to get a better idea of the temperature. And remember, New England will dish out any kind of weather it chooses. Your mantra should be "expect anything and be ready for everything."

| CONNECTICUT | | | |
|---|---|---|---|
| **MONTH** | **HIGH TEMP** | **LOW TEMP** | **AVERAGE PRECIPITATION (Rain or snow)** |
| January | 35.6°F | 17°F | $3^{53}/_{64}$" |
| February | 38.3°F | 18.8°F | $3^{11}/_{32}$" |
| March | 46.9°F | 26.2°F | $4^{7}/_{16}$" |
| April | 57.9°F | 35.2°F | $4^{7}/_{64}$" |
| May | 68.5°F | 44.4°F | $4^{13}/_{64}$" |
| June | 77.5°F | 54.1°F | $4^{9}/_{32}$" |
| July | 81.1°F | 59.7°F | $4^{9}/_{64}$" |
| August | 79.8°F | 58.2°F | $4^{5}/_{64}$" |
| September | 71.9°F | 50°F | $4^{25}/_{64}$" |
| October | 61.8°F | 39.5°F | $4^{11}/_{64}$" |
| November | 49.8°F | 31.6°F | $4^{13}/_{32}$" |
| December | 40.2°F | 22.4°F | $4^{33}/_{64}$" |

## MASSACHUSETTS

| MONTH | HIGH TEMP | LOW TEMP | AVERAGE PRECIPITATION (Rain or snow) |
|---|---|---|---|
| January | 33.8°F | 15.8°F | $3^{49}/_{64}$" |
| February | 36.3°F | 17.6°F | $3^3/_8$" |
| March | 44.2°F | 25.7°F | $4^7/_{32}$" |
| April | 56.1°F | 35.2°F | $3^{63}/_{64}$" |
| May | 67.2°F | 44.9°F | $3^{59}/_{64}$" |
| June | 75.3°F | 53.9°F | $3^{13}/_{16}$" |
| July | 80.7°F | 59.7°F | $3^9/_{64}$" |
| August | 78.9°F | 58.2°F | $3^{15}/_{16}$" |
| September | 71.6°F | 50.7°F | $3^7/_8$" |
| October | 60.8°F | 39.9°F | $4^1/_{32}$" |
| November | 49.1°F | 31.6°F | $4^1/_4$" |
| December | 38.3°F | 21.3°F | $4^7/_{64}$" |

## VERMONT

| MONTH | HIGH TEMP | LOW TEMP | AVERAGE PRECIPITATION (Rain or snow) |
|---|---|---|---|
| January | 25.8°F | 5.1°F | $2^{61}/_{64}$" |
| February | 30°F | 7.5°F | $2^5/_8$" |
| March | 37.4°F | 17°F | $3^3/_{16}$" |
| April | 50.7°F | 29.1°F | $3^{23}/_{64}$" |
| May | 63.6°F | 38.8°F | $3^{57}/_{64}$" |
| June | 73.7°F | 49.8°F | $4^9/_{64}$" |
| July | 75.9°F | 52.7°F | $4^9/_{32}$" |
| August | 73.4°F | 49.8°F | $4^{13}/_{64}$" |
| September | 67.2°F | 44.9°F | $3^{51}/_{64}$" |
| October | 55°F | 34.1°F | $3^{57}/_{64}$" |
| November | 41.7°F | 25.5°F | $3^{13}/_{16}$" |
| December | 31.1°F | 12.7°F | $3^{17}/_{32}$" |

| NEW HAMPSHIRE | | | |
|---|---|---|---|
| **MONTH** | **HIGH TEMP** | **LOW TEMP** | **AVERAGE PRECIPITATION (Rain or snow)** |
| January | 28.5°F | 8°F | $3^{1}/_{4}$" |
| February | 32.3°F | 10°F | $2^{15}/_{16}$" |
| March | 41°F | 19.9°F | $3^{41}/_{64}$" |
| April | 53.4°F | 30.7°F | $3^{5}/_{8}$" |
| May | 65.6°F | 41.1°F | $3^{27}/_{32}$" |
| June | 75°F | 51°F | $4^{3}/_{32}$" |
| July | 78.8°F | 55.5°F | $4^{3}/_{64}$" |
| August | 76.6°F | 53.6°F | $3^{7}/_{8}$" |
| September | 68.7°F | 45.6°F | $3^{23}/_{32}$" |
| October | 57.2°F | 35.6°F | $4^{1}/_{16}$" |
| November | 44.9°F | 26.9°F | $4^{1}/_{16}$" |
| December | 33.4°F | 15.2°F | $3^{3}/_{4}$" |

| MAINE | | | |
|---|---|---|---|
| **MONTH** | **HIGH TEMP** | **LOW TEMP** | **AVERAGE PRECIPITATION (RAIN OR SNOW)** |
| January | 26.2°F | 5.7°F | $3^{17}/_{64}$" |
| February | 29.8°F | 7.8°F | $2^{57}/_{64}$" |
| March | 38.4°F | 18.3°F | $3^{9}/_{16}$" |
| April | 50.7°F | 30.3°F | $3^{45}/_{64}$" |
| May | 63.5°F | 40.4°F | $3^{11}/_{16}$" |
| June | 72.8°F | 50.3°F | $3^{29}/_{32}$" |
| July | 77.9°F | 55.9°F | $3^{45}/_{64}$" |
| August | 76.2°F | 53.9°F | $3^{1}/_{2}$" |
| September | 67.2°F | 45.8°F | $3^{11}/_{16}$" |
| October | 55.7°F | 35.9°F | $4^{1}/_{8}$" |
| November | 43.1°F | 27.1°F | $4^{25}/_{64}$" |
| December | 31.8°F | 13.6°F | $3^{51}/_{64}$" |

For more detailed weather forecasting and historical data, check out the following sites:

★ **weather.com**      ★ **noaa.gov**

★ **usclimatedata.com**      ★ **weatherbase.com**

# Water

**HIKING ISN'T JUST FUN** and adventure and bonding with the outdoors. It's exercise. It's an aerobic activity. At the height of summer when it's hot out or when you're hiking up a particularly steep and rocky trail, you're going to know you're getting a workout. And just like during any other workout, you need to hydrate. Your body needs water to function properly. Always err on the side of caution when deciding how much water you will bring on a hike. And it's a good idea to bring means of water purification as well. It's better to return with a half-full water bottle than to run out halfway back.

How much water is enough? Here's a simple physiological fact that should convince you to bring a sufficient quantity when deciding how much water to pack: A hiker walking steadily in 90°F heat needs approximately 10 quarts of fluid per day. That's 2.5 gallons.

A good rule of thumb is to hydrate prior to your hike, carry and drink 6 ounces of water for every mile you plan to hike, and hydrate again after the hike. For most people, the pleasures of hiking make carrying water a relatively minor price to pay to remain safe and healthy. So pack more water than you think you'll need, even for short hikes.

And don't just bring a more-than-adequate supply of water. Be truly prepared and bring some means of water purification. If you're tempted to use water from streams, rivers, or lakes, do so with extreme caution. In fact, don't do it at all, unless you are carrying some means of purifying that water. Bring either a water filter or iodine tablets. And seek out running water. Many ponds and lakes are fairly stagnant. The water is much more likely to contain intestinal parasites, and it will probably taste terrible.

Drinking water from lakes and streams without purifying presents serious yet easily avoidable risks for thirsty trekkers. *Giardia* parasites contaminate many water sources and cause the dreaded intestinal giardiasis that can last for weeks after ingestion. To learn more about *giardia* and other intestinal parasites that may be lurking in that cool, clear mountain stream, visit the Centers for Disease Control and Prevention website at **cdc.gov/parasites /giardia**.

If you effectively purify or treat the water, you should be safe. Boiling water for 2–3 minutes is always a safe measure for camping, but that's not always practical when you're on a day hike. Fear not because you have several other options, including a filtration pump and iodine tablets.

A filtration pump with a carbon filter will remove parasites, particulate matter, and bad tastes from water you find in the wild. Other methods, such as iodine tablets, can add a chemical taste to the water. While slightly unpleasant, the water should be safe to drink. As a precaution, carry some means of water purification to help in a pinch. It's better to have some purified water that tastes a little off than to risk dehydration or an intestinal parasite.

## Clothing

**NEW ENGLAND WEATHER** is notoriously fickle. As stated earlier, expect anything and be ready for everything. You need to dress for the current temperature and for what the temperature may become. You must also account for the fact that you'll be generating heat while hiking and will then cool down rapidly once you stop. That calls for a classic layering strategy, with a thin base layer that wicks moisture away from your skin. Wear synthetic layers over that base layer, and have sufficient layers for all possibilities.

Variable weather, unexpected trail conditions, fatigue, a hike that's longer or more strenuous than you thought, and an unfortunate wrong turn can individually or collectively turn a great outing into an uncomfortable one at best—and a life-threatening one at worst. Proper attire plays a key role in staying comfortable—and occasionally staying alive. Here are some helpful guidelines:

★ *Choose polypropylene, silk, or wool for maximum comfort* in all of your hiking attire—from shirts to shorts and socks and everything in between. Wear a base layer that wicks sweat away from your skin as you're hiking and you'll be much more comfortable. Cotton is fine for relaxing after your hike, but you won't be happy if you're wearing material that gets wet and stays wet.

★ *Always wear a hat or have one with you.* During the cooler months, make sure it's a fleece hat that can keep you warm when you're on the summit or cooling down. During the summer, make sure it's a broad-brimmed hat that offers sun protection.

★ *Be ready to layer up or down* as the day progresses and the mercury rises or falls. Today's outdoor wear makes layering easy, with such designs as jackets that convert to vests and pants with zip-off or button-up legs.

★ *Wear mid-height or full-size hiking boots,* depending on the nature of the hike. On hot days during the summer, you may be tempted to go hiking in open sandals or casual sneakers. That's not a good idea for several reasons. Your bones and arches need support, and your skin needs protection. And if you get through the day without stubbing your toe on a rock, it will be a miracle. Save the sandals for lounging around post-hike.

★ *Wear good hiking socks with those boots.* You want to cushion your feet from the impact of hiking on rocky surfaces and have socks that will keep your feet warm even if the socks become damp from either sweat or an unexpected dunk during a stream crossing.

★ *Don't leave raingear behind,* even if the weather is clear and sunny at the beginning of your hike. Pack a jacket that is breathable and either water resistant or waterproof. Investigate different choices at your local outdoors retailer. If you're a frequent hiker, you'll eventually have more than one raingear weight, material, and style in your closet to protect you in all seasons in your regional climate and hiking microclimates.

## Essential Gear

**EVEN FOR A DAY HIKE,** there are several items that you should always carry for your safety and comfort. There can always be variables, even for the best-planned hike on a relatively mellow trail in perfect weather. Always be prepared for an injury, inclement weather, or even to help another hiker who has had some trouble and is not as well prepared as you. The following is a list of essential items you should always have with you in your side pockets or in your pack:

★ *Extra food* (trail mix, granola bars, or other high-energy foods)

★ *Extra clothes* (raingear, warm hat, gloves, and change of socks and shirt)

★ *Space blanket or emergency blanket* (This can save someone who becomes hypothermic.)

★ *Flashlight or headlamp with extra bulb and batteries*

★ *Insect repellent* (For some areas and seasons, this is extremely vital.)

★ *Maps and a high-quality compass* (Even if you know the terrain from previous hikes, don't leave home without these tools. And, as previously noted, bring maps in addition to those in this guidebook, and consult your maps prior to the hike. If you are well versed in GPS usage, bring that as well. However, do not rely on it as your sole navigational tool. Your GPS battery can dwindle or fade completely, or you might not get a signal in mountainous terrain or dense forests. Be sure to compare its guidance with that of your maps.)

★ *Pocketknife/multitool*

★ *Sun protection, including sunglasses, lip balm, and sunscreen* (Note the expiration date on the tube or bottle; it's usually embossed on the top.)

★ *Water* (As emphasized more than once in this book, bring more than you think you will drink. Depending on your destination, you may want to bring a container and iodine or a filter for purifying water in case you run out.)

★ *Whistle* (This can be your best friend in an emergency if you're trying to help rescuers find you if you're incapacitated or otherwise unable to make yourself visible.)

★ *Windproof matches/lighter, as well as a fire starter*

★ *First-aid kit* (components described in the next section)

# First-Aid Kit

**ANY PARAMEDIC** or wilderness medical technician will tell you that the products listed here, in alphabetical order, are just the basics. The reality of hiking is that you can be out for a week of backpacking and acquire only a mosquito bite. Or you can hike for an hour, slip, and suffer an abrasion or broken bone. Fortunately, these items collapse into a very small and light space. You also may purchase convenient, prepackaged first-aid kits at your pharmacy or on the Internet at wilderness supply stores like REI or EMS or **backcountry.com.** You can also check commercially available first-aid kits to see what they carry when you're preparing your own.

★ Ace bandages or Spenco joint wraps

★ Antibiotic ointment *(Neosporin or the generic equivalent)*

★ Athletic tape

★ Band-Aids

★ Benadryl or the generic equivalent diphenhydramine *(in case of allergic reactions)*

★ Blister kit *(such as Moleskin/Spenco Second Skin)*

★ Butterfly-closure bandages

★ Epinephrine in a prefilled syringe *(This is typically by prescription only for people known to have severe allergic reactions to hiking occurrences, such as bee stings.)*

★ Gauze *(one roll and a half dozen 4-by-4-inch compress pads)*

★ Hydrogen peroxide or iodine

★ Ibuprofen or acetaminophen

★ Snakebite kit

Pack the items in a waterproof bag, such as a zip-top bag. Consider the nature of the terrain you intend to hike and the number of hikers in your party before you exclude any article cited above. A gentle stroll may not inspire you to carry a complete kit, but anything beyond that warrants precaution. When hiking alone, you should always be prepared for any medical need. If you are hiking with only one partner or with a group, one or more people in your party should be equipped with a complete first-aid kit.

# General Safety Tips

**THE FOLLOWING TIPS** may have the familiar ring of your mother's voice as you take note, but you should heed them as you always heeded your mother.

★ *Always let someone know where you'll be hiking and how long you expect to be gone.* It's a good idea to give that person a copy of your route, particularly if you are headed into any isolated area. Let them know when you return.

★ *Always sign in and out of any trail registers provided.* Don't hesitate to comment on the trail condition if space is provided. That's your opportunity to alert others to any problems you encounter.

★ *Do not count on a cell phone for your safety.* Reception may be spotty or nonexistent on the trail.

★ *Always carry food and water, even on a short hike.* And bring more water than you think you will need. That's one point that can never be overemphasized.

★ *Never be afraid to ask questions.* State forest and park employees are there to help. It's a lot easier to solicit advice before a problem occurs. It can help you avoid a mishap away from civilization when it's too late to amend an error.

★ *Stay on designated trails.* Even on the most clearly marked trails, there's usually a point where you have to stop and consider which direction you need to go. The Appalachian Trail is usually quite well marked and well-defined, but there are more remote areas where you may wonder where the trail is going. If you become disoriented, don't panic. As soon as you think you may be off track, stop, assess your current direction, and then retrace your steps to the point where you went astray. Using a map, a compass, and this book, and keeping in mind what you have passed thus far, reorient yourself, and trust your judgment on which way to continue. If you become absolutely unsure of how to continue, return to your vehicle the way you came in. Should you become completely lost and have no idea how to find the trailhead, remaining in place along the trail and waiting for help is most often the best option for adults and always the best option for children.

★ *Always carry a whistle.* This is an exceptionally important precaution. It can be a lifesaver if you become lost or sustain an injury.

★ *Several of the hikes presented here have a significant stream cross-ing at the beginning or end of the hike (or both).* Be especially careful when crossing streams. Whether you're fording the stream, hopping from rock to rock, or crossing on a log, make every step count. If you have any doubt about maintaining your balance on a log, ford the stream instead. Use a trekking pole or stout stick for balance and face upstream as you cross. If a stream seems too deep to ford, turn back. Whatever is on the other side is not worth risking your life.

★ *Be particularly careful at overlooks.* There are many small clearings at the edge of a cliff throughout New England. While these ledges provide spectacular views, they are potentially hazardous. Stay back from the edge of outcrops, and make absolutely sure of your footing. A misstep can mean a nasty and possibly fatal fall.

★ *Standing dead trees and storm-damaged live trees pose a significant hazard to hikers.* These trees may have loose or broken limbs that could fall at any time. While walking beneath trees, and when choos-ing a spot to rest or enjoy your snack, look up and look around. Also be extremely careful if you're reaching for a tree or limb to help you up a steep section. Test it with partial weight before committing to using it to help you move.

★ *Know the symptoms of subnormal body temperature known as hypo-thermia.* Shivering and forgetfulness are the two most common indi-cators of this stealthy killer. Hypothermia can occur at any elevation, even in the summer, especially when the hiker is wearing lightweight cotton clothing. If symptoms present themselves, get to shelter, hot liquids, and dry clothes as soon as possible. The three stages are sometimes referred to as the fumbles, mumbles, and stumbles. As hypothermia gets progressively worse, you may have trouble per-forming simple tasks—the fumbles. As it advances, you may have trouble speaking clearly—the mumbles. At more advanced and more dangerous stages, you can have difficulty walking—the stumbles.

★ *Know the symptoms of heat exhaustion (hyperthermia).* Two early indicators are light-headedness and loss of energy. If you feel either or both of these symptoms, find some shade, drink some water, remove as many layers of clothing as practical, and stay put until you cool down. Marching through heat exhaustion can lead to heat-stroke—which can be fatal. If you should be sweating and you're not, that's another classic warning sign. Your hike is over at that point. Heatstroke is a life-threatening condition that can cause seizures, convulsions, and eventually death. If you or a companion reaches that point, do whatever you can to cool the victim down and seek medical attention immediately.

★ *Most important of all, don't forget to take along your brain.* A cool, calculating mind is your single-most important asset on the trail. Think before you act.

★ *Plan ahead.* Watch your step. Avoid accidents before they happen. Hiking is not an inherently dangerous activity, but a modicum of caution can ensure you enjoy a rewarding and relaxing hike.

# Animal, Insect, & Plant Hazards

## Black Bears

Though attacks by black bears are uncommon, the sight or approach of a bear can give anyone a start. If you encounter a bear while hiking, remain calm and avoid running in any direction. Make loud noises to scare off the bear and back away slowly. In primitive and remote areas, you can assume bears will be present. Check on the current bear situation or any recent bear activity prior to hiking.

Most encounters are food related, as bears have an exceptional sense of smell and not particularly discriminating tastes. While this is of greater concern to backpackers and campers, on a day hike you may have a lunchtime picnic or munch on a power bar or other snack from time to time. Remain aware and alert, and you should be able to avoid any problems.

## Black Flies

Though certainly a pest and maddening annoyance, the worst a black fly will cause is an itchy welt. They are most active mid-May–June, during the day, and especially before thunderstorms, as well as during the morning and evening hours. Insect repellent has some effect, though the only way to keep out of their swarming midst is to keep moving.

## Mosquitoes

Mosquitoes can turn a great day of hiking into an uncomfortable experience. Ward off these pests with insect repellent or repellent-impregnated clothing. In some areas, mosquitoes could even be carrying the West Nile virus, so use all sorts of caution to avoid mosquito bites.

## Poison Ivy, Oak, & Sumac

Recognizing and avoiding poison ivy, oak, and sumac are the most effective ways to prevent the painful, itchy rashes associated with these plants. Poison ivy occurs as a vine or ground cover, three leaflets to a leaf. Poison oak occurs as either a vine or shrub, also with three leaflets. Poison sumac flourishes in swampland, each leaf having 7–13 leaflets.

Urushiol, the oil in the sap of these plants, is responsible for the rash. Within 14 hours of exposure, raised lines/blisters will appear on the affected area, accompanied by a terrible itch. Refrain from scratching because bacteria under your fingernails can cause an infection. Wash and dry the affected area thoroughly, applying a calamine lotion to help dry out the rash. If itching or blistering is severe, seek medical attention. If you do come into contact with one of these plants, remember that oil-contaminated clothes, hiking gear, and pets can easily cause an irritating rash on you or someone else, so wash not only any exposed parts of your body but also any exposed clothes, gear, and pets.

## Snakes

Rattlesnakes and copperheads are among the most common venomous snakes in the United States and the ones you are likely to encounter in New England. It is unlikely, but you could encounter any of these varieties of venomous snakes in New England. Hibernation season is typically October–April. Rattlesnakes like to bask in the sun and won't bite unless threatened. They're most typically found in rocky areas. Cottonmouths are most often found in marshy or wetland areas.

The snakes you will most likely see while hiking will be nonvenomous species and subspecies. The best rule is to leave all snakes alone, give them a wide berth as you hike past, and make sure any hiking companions (including dogs) do the same.

When hiking, stick to well-used trails, and wear over-the-ankle boots and loose-fitting long pants. Do not step or put your hands beyond your range of detailed visibility, and avoid wandering around in the dark. Step onto logs and rocks, never over them, and be especially careful when climbing rocks. Always avoid walking through dense brush or willow thickets.

## Ticks

Ticks are often found on brush and tall grass, where they seem to be waiting to hitch a ride on a warm-blooded passerby. Adult ticks are most active April–May and again October–November. Among the varieties of ticks, the black-legged tick, commonly called the deer tick, is the primary carrier of Lyme disease. And the nymph, or baby, deer ticks are the most toxic.

Wear light-colored clothing, making it easier for you to spot ticks before they migrate to your skin. At the end of the hike, visually check your hair, back of neck, armpits, and socks. During your post-hike shower, take a moment to do a more complete body check. If you find one, don't panic. It typically takes 24–48 hours of having the tick embedded to transfer any toxins. Check for the classic bull's-eye-shaped rash. For ticks that are already embedded, removal with tweezers is best. Use disinfectant solution on the wound. Check with your doctor if you have any doubts. If you fear you have contracted anything, a round of antibiotics can often prevent further infection.

# Hunting

**SEPARATE RULES,** regulations, and licenses govern the various hunting types and related seasons. Though there are generally no problems, hikers may wish to forgo their trips during the big-game seasons, usually in November and December, when the woods suddenly seem filled with orange and camouflage. While hunting is not allowed in national parks, it is allowed on other lands along the

Appalachian Trail. Hunters tend to approach the trail from the sides, not the trailheads, and may not know that they are in prohibited zones, so it is always best to exercise caution.

# Regulations

**IN PLACES WHERE THE APPALACHIAN TRAIL** passes through national or state forest lands, please check with the local authorities if you have any questions. See Appendix A for contact information.

# Trail Etiquette

**ALWAYS TREAT THE TRAIL,** wildlife, and fellow hikers with respect. Here are some reminders:

★ *Plan ahead* in order to be self-sufficient at all times. Carry all necessary supplies for changes in weather or other conditions. A well-planned trip will be rewarding and safe for you and your companions.

★ *Hike on open trails only.*

★ *In seasons or construction areas* where road or trail closures may be a possibility, use the website addresses shown in the "Contact" line for each of this guidebook's hikes to check conditions prior to heading out for your hike. Do not attempt to circumvent such closures.

★ *Avoid trespassing on private land.* Obtain all permits and authorization as required. Also, leave gates as you find them or as directed by signage.

★ *Be courteous to others you encounter on the trails.*

★ *Never spook wild animals or pets.* An unannounced approach, a sudden movement, or a loud noise can startle most wild critters. A surprised animal can be dangerous to you, to others, and to the animal itself. Give wild animals plenty of space.

★ *Observe the yield signs* around the region's trailheads and backcountry. Be courteous to other trail users. Most sections of the Appalachian Trail are restricted to hikers, but you may encounter other trail users. Typically hikers should yield to horses, and bikers yield to both horses and hikers. By common courtesy on hills, hikers and bikers yield to any uphill traffic. When encountering mounted riders or horse packers, hikers should courteously step off the trail, on the downhill side if possible. Position yourself so the horse can see and hear you. Calmly greet the riders before they reach you and don't dart behind trees. Also resist the urge to pet horses unless you are invited to do so.

★ *Stay on the existing trail.* Don't blaze any new trails.

★ *Be sure to pack out what you pack in.* Take only pictures and memories. Leave only footprints. No one likes to see the trash someone else has left behind.

Familiarize yourself with and adhere to the principles of Leave No Trace (**lnt.org**). You can find A.T.-specific guidelines at **appalachian trail.org/lnt.**

# Tips on Enjoying Hiking in New England

**AS STATED EARLIER,** expect anything and be prepared for everything. What makes hiking on the Appalachian Trail in New England a spectacularly beautiful experience can also make it a challenge. Be ready for any changes in weather, changes in plans that may require extra gear, and changes in terrain that may require a change of plans.

Keep these suggestions in mind, plan ahead, and prepare properly and thoroughly, and you will have the experience of a lifetime. There are some beautiful and dramatic day hikes on the Appalachian Trail as it winds through New England. Enjoy your time on this fabled footpath.

OPPOSITE: AT SEVERAL SPOTS ON THE APPALACHIAN TRAIL, SUCH AS MAPLE HILL, YOU ARE AT THE MERCY OF THE GRANITE. *(See page 113.)*

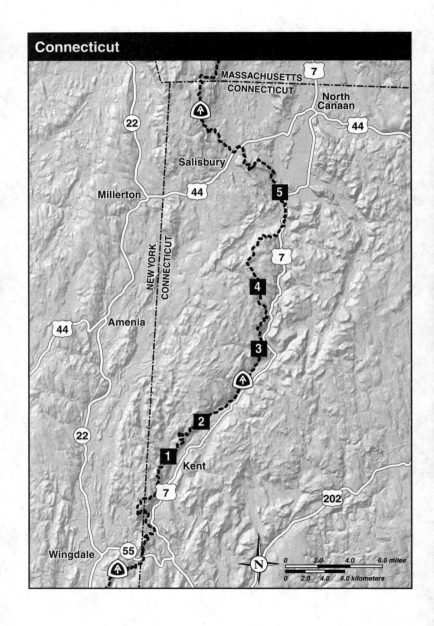

# Connecticut

**THE MOUNT PROSPECT TRAIL TAKES YOU PAST GREAT FALLS.** *(See page 48.)*

# Mount Algo

SCENERY: ★ ★ ★
TRAIL CONDITION: ★ ★ ★
CHILDREN: ★ ★ ★
DIFFICULTY: ★ ★ ★
SOLITUDE: ★ ★ ★

**THE LOOSE FOREST ON MOUNT ALGO ALLOWS LOTS OF LIGHT TO THE FOREST FLOOR.**

**GPS TRAILHEAD COORDINATES:** N41° 43.864' W73° 29.439'

**DISTANCE & CONFIGURATION:** 2-mile out-and-back

**HIKING TIME:** 2.5 hours

**HIGHLIGHTS:** Scenic, short, steep hike

**ELEVATION:** 1,370' at summit, 470' at trailhead

**ACCESS:** Unrestricted (trail open 24/7, no fees), roadside parking for three or four vehicles

**MAPS:** Appalachian Trail Conservancy *MA–CT Map 4* and DeLorme *CT RI Atlas & Gazetteer Map 40*

**CONTACT:** Connecticut chapter of Appalachian Mountain Club: **ct-amc.org**

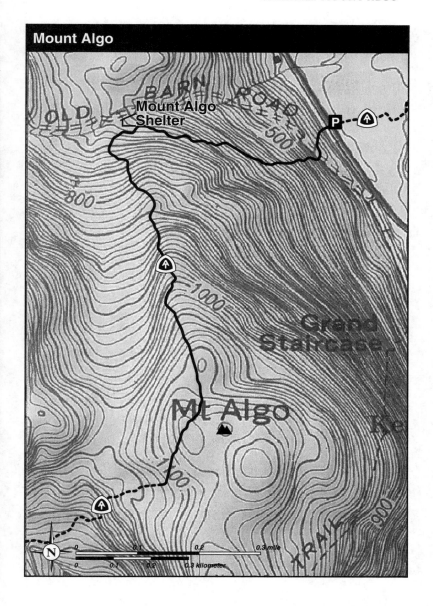

Mount Algo

## Overview

Mount Algo is a classic New England drumlin. It's quite steep in spots as you ascend the side but then much more flat and rounded near the top. There's not much of a defined peak and no real views to speak of, but it's a pleasant, surprisingly aggressive, and rocky hike.

## Route Details

If there were one phrase to describe most of the Appalachian Trail hikes in southern New England, it would be short and steep. Mount Algo is certainly no exception to that. The trailhead is right off the road, on the left as you're heading west out of Kent, Connecticut, on CT 341. To the right, there is a small footbridge over which hikers can cross a small electric fence encircling the field on the north side of the road. From there, the trail continues up through the rest of New England and on to Katahdin.

The trail starts off quite steeply, even just feet from the trail-head on the road. If you need to warm up, you might want to do it before you actually hit the trail. The trail continues to ascend quickly through a fairly dense forest of mixed deciduous and coniferous trees, with moderate levels of undergrowth. The trail surface is uneven and rocky right off the bat, and it stays that way.

While the trail is fairly well marked by the white blazes early on in this section, it's not all that well-defined. Keep your eyes open

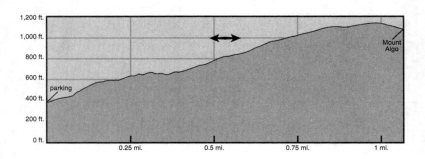

for the series of white blazes to ensure that you do indeed stay on the trail. After about 10 minutes into the hike, the trail crosses over an old fire road. The Appalachian Trail is across the road and down about 20 feet or so.

After crossing over the fire road, the trail winds to the right. It continues its steep and rocky ascent. Considering the steep pitch of the trail and the rocky trail surface, this trail may not be suitable for the youngest hikers. Bring along the kids, but only if they already have some hiking experience. Because the trail maintains a moderate pitch in this section, it's good to see well-constructed water bars made of overlapped flat rocks.

The trail surface here is quite rocky, so watch your step. The trail flattens out a bit as it crosses over the remnants of an old stone wall. It almost feels like you're hiking along a ridgeline here, as the trail follows a long switchback to the right. As you continue to gain altitude following the consistently aggressive ascent, the views to the north begin to emerge through the trees.

The trail continues to follow the ridgeline to the west. The trail surface is still quite rocky here, so proper hiking footwear is essential. After the initial elevation gain and a relatively consistent climb for approximately 20 minutes, the trail gives you a break and the grade softens briefly. Shortly after that respite, the trail pitch becomes more moderate. At this point, the white-blazed Appalachian Trail intersects with the blue-blazed state trail. There's also a sign here for the Mount Algo shelter.

The trail winds around to the left here and once again begins to steepen. The trail passes through a dramatically scenic open grove of tall maples and beech trees. The trail is very well-defined here as it cuts through the forest. The trail continues to gain in pitch as the switchback continues. The trail continues east, climbing more steeply along the ridgeline. The forest gets denser and the trees taller as the trail winds to the right and heads in a more southerly direction.

The trail is more well-defined here by the dense forest and undergrowth on both sides. After moving through the dense undergrowth and coming up over a brief rise, the trail flattens out a bit as you near the summit of Mount Algo. As the trail veers a bit to the right and south, it pitches up for the final stretch.

Right near to the top of Mount Algo, the trail becomes a bit steeper and rockier. There's almost a false summit here before you get to the real top. You make your way up through a very scenic natural rock garden toward the final few paces to the summit. At the summit, which isn't really all that well-defined, there are large boulders on either side of the trail. This is often the case with these smaller, southern New England mountains. You might not even realize you've made it to the top until you start descending on the other side. Nevertheless, the summit plateau of Mount Algo is marked by those two good-size boulders on either side of the trail.

Mount Algo is a classic New England drumlin—steep on the sides and fairly flat and rounded at the top where the glaciers shaved off the rest of the peak during the last ice age. The Mount Algo hike is a relatively steep hike in certain portions to the fairly rounded summit, with a nice spot to stop at the top for lunch or a snack break before heading back down the trail.

## Nearby Attractions

The town of Kent, Connecticut, is right nearby. It's a fairly quiet town but a pleasant place to visit after hiking. You will also be fairly close to Danbury, Connecticut, if you need more options for lodging or dining.

## Directions

From US 7 in Kent, Connecticut, follow CT 341 (also called Macedonia Road) west 1 mile. The small roadside parking area will be on the left. You'll see a wooden footbridge on the right that crosses over a wire fence. The parking and trailhead are right across the street.

**2** # St. Johns Ledges

ST. JOHNS LEDGES IS AN IMPRESSIVELY STEEP
AND MASSIVE ROCK LEDGE.

SCENERY: ★ ★ ★ ★ ★
TRAIL CONDITION: ★ ★ ★
CHILDREN: ★ ★ ★
DIFFICULTY: ★ ★ ★
SOLITUDE: ★ ★ ★

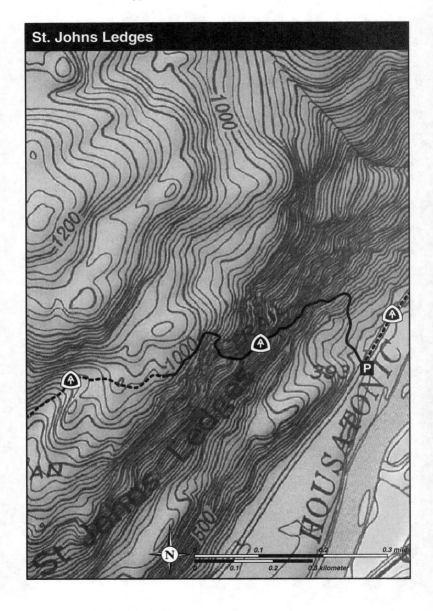

St. Johns Ledges

**GPS TRAILHEAD COORDINATES:** N41° 46.059' W73° 26.473'

**DISTANCE & CONFIGURATION:** 1.2-mile out-and-back

**HIKING TIME:** 1.25 hours

**HIGHLIGHTS:** Dramatic views from atop ledges

**ELEVATION:** 1,050' at summit, 364' at trailhead

**ACCESS:** Unrestricted (trail open 24/7, no fees), trailhead parking off River Road

**MAPS:** Appalachian Trail Conservancy *MA–CT Map 4* and DeLorme *CT RI Atlas & Gazetteer Map 40*

**CONTACT:** Connecticut chapter of Appalachian Mountain Club: **ct-amc.org**

## Overview

The rock scramble up the side of St. Johns Ledge is like a mini Hunt Spur on Katahdin. This short but intense hike leads you to some impressive views of Housatonic Valley.

## Route Details

The hike up and over St Johns Ledges is short, steep, and dramatic. The views of the cliff as you're climbing along the side and the views of the valley when you reach the top are worth the challenging scramble over the rocks.

From the trailhead parking area, head south on the Appalachian Trail (A.T.) away from the Housatonic River. The trail starts off with a steady, moderate ascent through a loose mixed forest of maple and birch. The trail surface is slightly rocky, some of which may be a bit loose, so step carefully, as always.

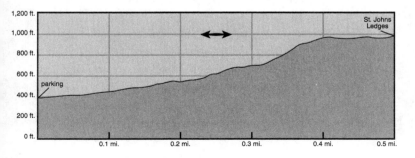

35

At first, the trail follows a moderate rolling grade. Looking up into the woods toward the massive ledges facing you, you know that will change soon. Sure enough, after a few minutes the trail picks up to a steady ascent. The trail is quite well marked and well-defined here. After about 5 minutes, the trail takes a sharp turn to the left (south) and continues its sustained moderate climb. The trail is a little uneven here with lots of roots and rocks.

As the trail climbs closer to the massive rock ledges, it starts growing steeper and the trail surface rockier. You'll come to a couple of stone staircases along the way. As you get closer, you start getting dramatic views of this massive granite ledge through the trees. This ledge is so steep and precipitous that it's a popular destination for rock climbers. Don't be surprised if you see some climbers ascending the ledge or rappelling down.

After about 10 minutes of hiking, the trail is now steep and steady. You'll pass directly beneath the first of several smaller rock ledges before coming to the largest ledge. The trail becomes extremely steep, rocky, and uneven directly beneath the ledge. Even though the rock formations are dramatic and scenic, watch your step, as the footing can be treacherous. You'll need to be equally cautious on the way up and the way down.

Continue following the steep, rocky, and uneven trail as it winds its way along the base of the ledges. It's fairly well marked here, if not as well-defined because of all the rock scrambling you'll be doing. After about 20 minutes, you'll be doing some hand-over-hand scrambling up the rocks. It's more like nontechnical rock climbing than hiking in this section.

After following along the base of the ledge, the trail will follow up the far side on the south. This is like a smaller cousin to the Hunt Spur on Katahdin. You are definitely in for some hand-over-hand scrambling here and climbing up steep, uneven stone stairways. Take your time in here because it's strenuous, uneven footing and quite dramatically beautiful, so take a look around when you stop to catch your breath.

After about 30 minutes into the hike, you'll be finished with the rock-climbing portion of the trail. The trail resumes its steady steep ascent up over the top of the ledges. Here you'll pass through a grove of young maple and birch. It's a nice rest after the aggressive climbing it took to get here. Then the trail heads south, bearing to the left. Hiking along the ridgetop as you are here, the trail pitch relaxes somewhat, but don't relax too much yourself.

Pay careful attention to where you're hiking and your position. You are completely atop St. Johns Ledges now, and a fall to the left would likely be fatal. Step slowly and carefully. When the trail starts rolling downward slightly, keep an eye on the left for an opening in the trees and the small wooden sign proclaiming St. Johns Ledges. The view from here is intense. Kick back and relax on the rocks, and congratulate yourself on completing this short but impressively steep climb.

From here, you can enjoy the sweeping views of the Housatonic Valley or continue on to Caleb's Peak to extend the hike, if you wish. And again, be equally careful, if not more so, as you navigate your way down the rock ledges down the side of the main open ledge. You do not want to slip here.

## Nearby Attractions

The town of Kent, Connecticut, is right nearby. It's a fairly quiet town, but a pleasant place to visit after hiking. You will also be fairly close to Danbury, Connecticut, if you need more options for lodging or dining.

## Directions

From US 7 in Kent, Connecticut, follow CT 341 across the Housatonic River 0.3 mile to Skiff Mountain Road. Turn right, and follow it 1 mile to River Road (a dirt road off to the right following the Housatonic River). Follow River Road for about 2.5 miles to a small parking area on the left. You'll see a sign for the A.T.

# Pine Knob

SCENERY: ★ ★ ★
TRAIL CONDITION: ★ ★ ★ ★
CHILDREN: ★ ★ ★ ★
DIFFICULTY: ★ ★
SOLITUDE: ★ ★ ★ ★

**THE PINE KNOB TRAIL IS A RELAXING RAMBLE THROUGH THE WOODS.**

**GPS TRAILHEAD COORDINATES:** N41° 49.378' W73° 23.198'

**DISTANCE & CONFIGURATION:** 2.6-mile out-and-back

**HIKING TIME:** 2.25 hours

**HIGHLIGHTS:** Sweeping views from just below top

**ELEVATION:** 1,350' at summit, 650' at trailhead

**ACCESS:** Unrestricted (trail open 24/7, no fees), parking off CT 4 or another trailhead parking lot on US 7

**MAPS:** Appalachian Trail Conservancy *MA–CT Maps 3 and 4* and DeLorme *CT RI Atlas & Gazetteer Map 40*

**CONTACT:** Connecticut chapter of Appalachian Mountain Club: **ct-amc.org**

## Pine Knob

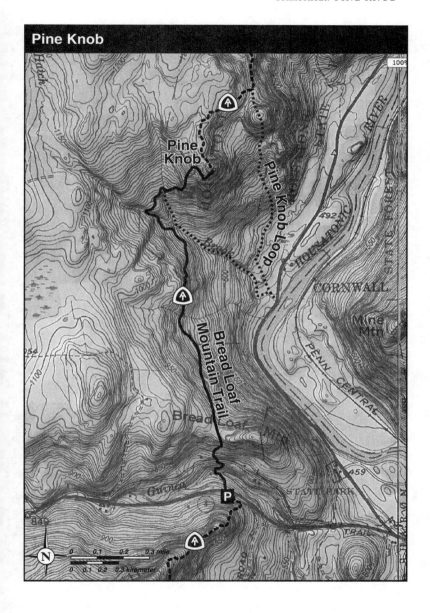

## Overview

After a steep initial climb, Pine Knob Loop Trail rolls up and down on its way to the rounded summit with dramatic views of the Housatonic Valley.

## Route Details

The Pine Knob hike is a beautiful ramble through the Connecticut forest. It can be a bit tough to find, and parking is tight. There are just a few spots alongside CT 4 right across the road from the Appalachian Trail (A.T.) sign. There's also a trailhead parking area down off US 7, just north of the intersection of US 7 and CT 4. This is for the Norwalk Trail, from which you can intersect with the A.T.

Be extremely careful crossing CT 4. Cars come zooming up that hill. The trail winds down into the forest right off CT 4. It's very well marked and well-defined here. The trail descends to the edge of Guinea Brook. The hill leading down to the brook is quite steep and can be wet, so watch your step. Guinea Brook is not too deep, but it is wide. If it seems unsafe to pass here, do not attempt. Follow CT 4 east (down the hill) to Old Sharon Road, which will be a hairpin turn to the left. Hike up this road about 0.3 mile to where the A.T. crosses.

If you do take the Guinea Brook route, after crossing, the trail zigs and zags up the hillside. It's an abrupt steep-but-short climb on a smooth, firm trail. After this short, steep climb, you'll cross over Old Sharon Road (a dirt road).

After crossing over Old Sharon Road, the trail climbs steeply through the loose mixed forest of mostly birch and maple trees. This steep initial climb also takes you over a couple of sets of stone staircases. Halfway up the hillside, the trail becomes quite rocky. Here you are also approaching a dramatic rock ledge. Keep an eye on the white blazes here, as it would be easy to wander off-trail. You're hiking through and over the loosely spaced rocks below this massive granite ledge. This part of the trail is impressively steep and rocky but of relatively short duration. You'll arrive at the top of the ledge after 25 minutes or so.

Toward the top, the A.T. winds around to the left of this rock ledge. You'll have a dramatic view looking downhill here. At this point, the A.T. intersects with the Bread Loaf Mountain Trail with a 0.1-mile trail to the summit or 0.6 mile to the US 7 trailhead parking. Follow the A.T. off to the left.

Here the trail mellows out considerably, which is a nice break after that initial steep lunge. The trail is also much better defined and marked here. If you do take the Old Sharon bypass and avoid the Guinea Brook crossing, this would be a good hike with kids. The forest is spectacularly open and breezy in this area. It's still mostly maple and birch, which impart a brilliant color to the forest in all seasons. At 35 minutes into the hike, the trail continues its gentle ramble, rising and falling through the forest.

After about 45 minutes, you'll come to a short stream crossing. The trail gets a bit rockier after this, but this is still a mellow hike. Shortly after the stream, the trail begins a mellow ascent toward another rock ledge. The trail pitches up just a bit below the ledge, and you actually climb up and over this small ledge.

At the top of the ledge, there's a significant quartz deposit. You'll see large quartz chunks all over the ground atop this ledge. It's quite a dramatic sight, especially when set against the leaves blanketing the forest floor.

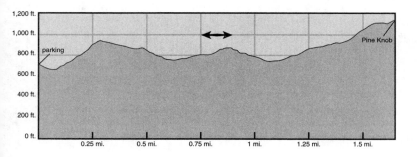

The trail descends quite steeply off the back of this ledge, so step carefully. There's also a sharp drop to the right. After this steep descent and passing along another rock ledge, the trail continues its gentle ascent. You're at almost 1 hour into the hike at this point. Now the trail descends toward a stream running through the base of a fairly large and gently sloping gully. The trail heads toward the stream, then back up the hill to the left. The trail briefly gets a bit rockier and steeper here.

After running parallel to the stream for a bit, the trail crosses over. It is a fairly easy crossing, with a nice trail of large boulders leading you across. After this crossing and at the 1-hour-and-10-minute mark, the A.T. intersects and overlaps with the blue-blazed Pine Knob Loop Trail. Now you're following white and blue blazes. The trail gets fairly steep after this intersection, then zigs and zags up the hillside for the final push to the top of Pine Knob.

At 1 hour and 20 minutes, you'll come to a dramatic rock ledge on the right with views of the surrounding forest and the Housatonic Valley. The actual top of the rounded Pine Knob summit plateau is just a few minutes farther along, but this overlook is where you'll want to stay.

## Nearby Attractions

The town of Kent, Connecticut, is just to the south, as is Macedonia Brook State Park and the numerous areas of Wyantenock State Forest.

## Directions

From US 7 in Kent, Connecticut, go north about 9.7 miles, and turn left onto CT 4 West toward Sharon. In 0.6 mile, there is limited trailhead parking on the left (south) side of CT 4. Alternate trailhead parking is available near the intersection of CT 4 and US 7.

# Mount Easter

SCENERY: ★ ★ ★
TRAIL CONDITION: ★ ★ ★ ★
CHILDREN: ★ ★ ★
DIFFICULTY: ★ ★ ★
SOLITUDE: ★ ★ ★ ★

NOT LONG INTO MOUNT EASTER TRAIL, YOU GO THROUGH A MASSIVE SPLIT GRANITE LEDGE.

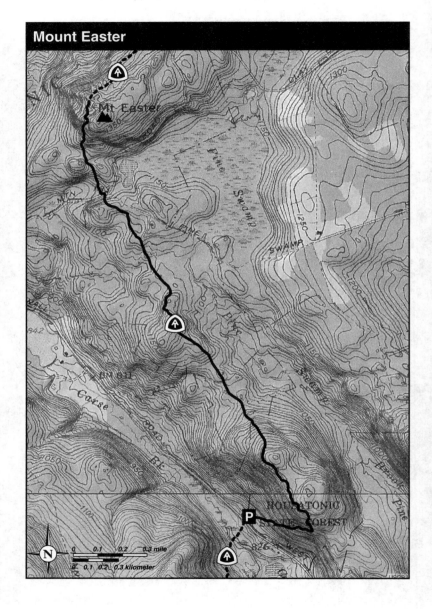

Mount Easter

**GPS TRAILHEAD COORDINATES:** N41° 52.392' W73° 23.476'

**DISTANCE & CONFIGURATION:** 4.8-mile out-and-back

**HIKING TIME:** 2.5 hours

**HIGHLIGHTS:** Impressive views from atop rock ledge

**ELEVATION:** 1,391' at summit, 841' at trailhead

**ACCESS:** Limited parking at trailhead on West Cornwall Road

**MAPS:** Appalachian Trail Conservancy *MA–CT Map 3* and DeLorme *CT RI Atlas & Gazetteer Map 49*

**CONTACT:** Connecticut chapter of Appalachian Mountain Club: **ct-amc.org**

## Overview

The Mount Easter trail starts with a steep, rocky climb, even taking you through a notch in a massive granite ledge. Then it's a relatively mellow ramble along the ridgeline with fantastic views.

## Route Details

The trailhead can be a little tough to find. Follow the West Cornwall Road for a mile or so, then keep a sharp eye out for a white blaze in the woods. There's no real sign at the trailhead. There's a small pulloff with space for four or five cars on the left side of the road and a single yellow blaze on a tree.

The trailhead for Mount Easter is across the street from the parking area. The narrow trail begins a moderate ascent as soon as you enter the woods. The trail surface is firm, hard-packed dirt, and

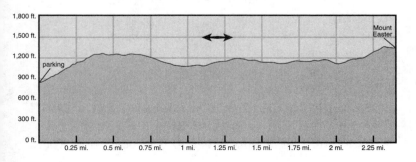

you're hiking through a loosely spaced forest of mostly birch and maple. There's also a loose undergrowth of young saplings.

Not too long into the hike, the trail surface gets rocky as the trail continues its steady moderate ascent. The trail veers to the right and continues climbing. Then you come to the first stone staircase of the hike. You're gaining elevation fairly quickly in this initial section. The trail continues its relatively straight hillside traverse.

At about 10 minutes into the hike, you'll come to the base of a dramatic rock ledge. The trail passes below the ledges and in and around some larger boulders. Then, at the 15-minute mark, the trail passes directly through a massive crack in one of the larger parts of this huge granite ledge. It's quite a dramatic part of the trail. You're still climbing, but up through this split in the giant rock ledge. With a pack on, it's just barely wide enough to pass through without turning sideways.

As you work your way up through this gap, which is anywhere from 2 to 4 feet wide, there are plenty of handholds and footholds to make your way. Once you emerge at the top of the gap, you are also atop most of the rock ledge. You can start to see the hillsides to the south through the treetops.

As you near the true top of this massive rock ledge, the trail veers sharply to the left (west). It's very rocky going here, so watch your step. You'll also pass by a nice clearing with more dramatic views to the south. The trail here is quite well marked and well-defined. After 25 minutes, you'll come off the rock ledges and back onto hard-packed trail meandering through the forest. The moderate grade is a nice break after scrambling up through that ledge gap. The forest here is still loose and airy, with nice breezes blowing through as you arrive atop the ridgeline.

After some more up and down atop the ridgeline, after about 40 minutes, the trail begins a moderate descent. After a short distance, it flattens out again. The trail remains well-defined and well marked here. Then, after another brief ramble, you'll pass the short spur trail for the Pine Swamp shelter. At this point, you're about halfway to the top of Mount Easter. After passing the shelter, the trail continues its gentle ramble through the forest.

The trail rises and falls along the top of the ridgeline for most of the latter half of the hike. After 1 hour and 15 minutes, you'll cross over a dirt fire road. Head straight across this road to stay on the Appalachian Trail. After crossing the road, the trail maintains a moderate grade with a slightly steeper climb. About 5 minutes later, you'll come out on another older fire road bed. The trail follows this briefly, then veers to the right back into the forest.

Here you'll find a final steeper pitch as you approach the top of Mount Easter. The pitch after passing the two fire roads is steeper and the trail surface much rockier in this final push to the top. When you do reach the top, there's a fairly decent view, as the summit is still heavily wooded. There are also some nice rocks upon which to perch for a lunch break before heading down.

## Nearby Attractions

Housatonic State Forest is nearby, but there aren't any large towns or cities.

## Directions

From US 7 in West Cornwall, Connecticut, follow the steep, winding West Cornwall Road 2.2 miles to the trailhead. If you pass Miles Pond on the left or Mount Easter Road on the right, you've gone too far.

SCENERY: ★ ★ ★ ★
TRAIL CONDITION: ★ ★ ★ ★
CHILDREN: ★ ★ ★ ★
DIFFICULTY: ★ ★ ★
SOLITUDE: ★ ★ ★

**NOT ALL THE WHITE BLAZES ARE ON TREES OR ROCKS, ESPECIALLY ON THE MOUNT PROSPECT TRAIL.**

**GPS TRAILHEAD COORDINATES:** N41° 57.351' W73° 22.073'

**DISTANCE & CONFIGURATION:** 6.2-mile out-and-back

**HIKING TIME:** 1.75 hours

**HIGHLIGHTS:** Great Falls

**ELEVATION:** 1,475' at summit, 1,050' at trailhead

**ACCESS:** Unrestricted (trail open 24/7, no fees), large parking area in Falls Village

**MAPS:** Appalachian Trail Conservancy *MA–CT Map 3* and DeLorme *CT RI Atlas & Gazetteer Map 49*

**CONTACT:** Connecticut chapter of Appalachian Mountain Club: **ct-amc.org**

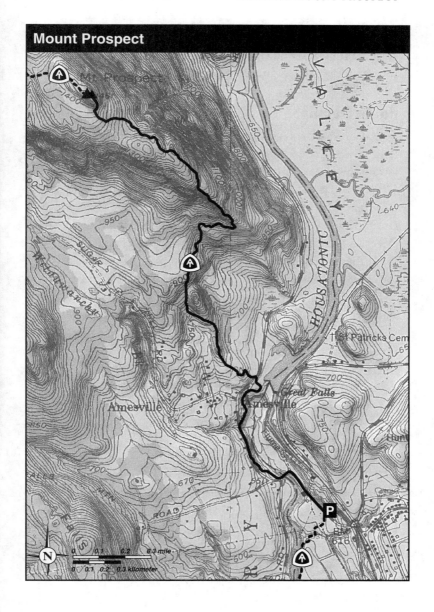

Mount Prospect

## Overview

The Mount Prospect trail takes you past the dramatic Great Falls and through some spectacularly scenic forest.

## Route Details

Mount Prospect is tucked away in western Connecticut. From the large parking area in Falls Village, walk toward the power station, following the blazes on the backs of telephone poles and road signs. White blazes aren't always painted on trees or rocks. You'll even see a blaze on the back of the street sign marking the end of Water Street. Once you've passed the power station and reached the end of Water Street, walk over the old metal bridge crossing the Housatonic River.

The trail finally enters the woods just past the metal bridge on the other side. Step off the bridge and look for the white blaze just off to the right. The trail is well-defined and well marked and takes you through dense undergrowth with a light, loosely spaced forest overhead. The trail surface here is sandy and hard packed and mostly flat for 50 yards or so. After that, you'll come to a Y-shaped intersection where the Appalachian Trail (A.T.) heads left uphill.

The trail here rises up away from the river but still generally follows the river's path. The trail is still quite well marked and defined here. About 15 minutes into the hike, the trail follows along the same course as a paved road. You actually walk up on the road, following the

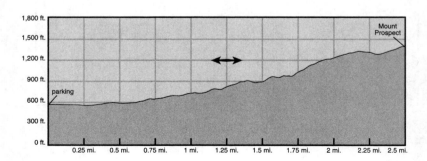

blazes on trees and telephone poles. When the road and trail cross a stone bridge, the trail reenters the woods, heading down to the right.

The trail is still following the high side of the riverbank, rising and falling but neither gaining nor losing much elevation. Fortunately, the Appalachian Trail is well marked here as it intersects with a few local walking paths. About 30 minutes into the hike, there's a detour to the right to Great Falls. It is definitely worth checking out this beautiful series of waterfalls.

When you return to the A.T. after gazing at the falls, the trail gets a bit more up and down and the trail surface gets a bit rougher with roots and rocks. In some spots, you're hiking over massive granite slabs—the same rock formations that make up the riverbed and the waterfalls. After passing the falls, the trail crosses a road. Go directly across the road and into the woods to stay on the A.T.

Once you're in the woods on the other side of the road, the trail begins a gentle, steady ascent on a nice, firm surface. The trail is clearly defined and marked here. While making this steady moderate ascent, you can still hear the roar of the falls as a background to the woodland birds. About 35 minutes into the hike, you come to a massive boulder on the left side of the trail.

After you pass the huge boulder, the trail descends and passes into an open field. You cross through one open field while steadily climbing. You move through a stand of trees into another open field and another after that. These fields and the trees that define their borders are truly quite scenic. And the trail maintains a steady, moderate ascent and reenters the forest.

About 45 minutes into the hike, the trail passes through an open grove with lots of fern as ground cover and tall slender trees making up the high forest canopy. The trail is still making a moderate, sustained climb with a firm, clean surface. A bit farther along, the trail follows along and through a large gorge and hillside. The open character of the forest here makes it quite a scenic hike.

One thing to note, as with many of New England's hiking trails: It is much more difficult to follow the trail in the fall when the ground is blanketed with leaves. Keep an eye on the white blazes, watch the trail at ground level, and you'll be OK.

You'll reach the rounded summit plateau at about 55 minutes into the hike. There's a large, open clearing that you can see through the trees to the left. While this may be the highest point, it's worth a little extra hiking to continue past this plateau for another 10 minutes or so, descending from the rounded hilltop to come around a bend to a more open, scenic overlook. This would be a good place to stop and enjoy the view and some cool breezes.

## Nearby Attractions

Housatonic State Forest is nearby, but there aren't any large towns or cities.

## Directions

From US 7 in West Cornwall, Connecticut, go north about 6.5 miles, and turn left onto CT 126 toward Falls Village. In 0.6 mile turn right onto Railroad Street, and then immediately turn left onto Water Street, following the signs for the falls and hiking and walking trails. A good-size parking area is off to the left just before the falls and the power station.

OPPOSITE: THE FOREST ON MOUNT PROSPECT IS
LUSH AND GREEN AND QUITE SCENIC.

# Massachusetts

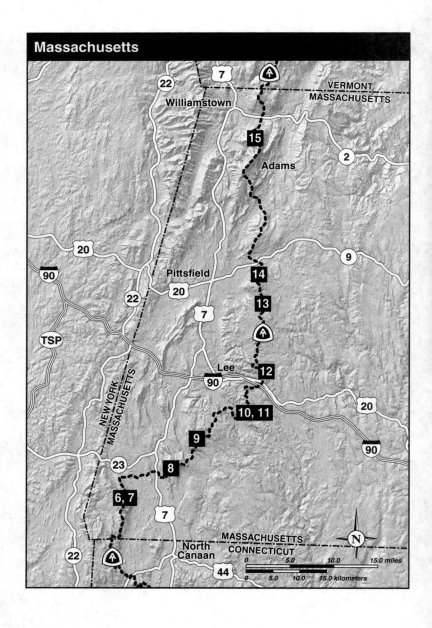

# Massachusetts

**A STEEP HIKE BRINGS YOU TO THE RIDGELINE OF JUG END STATE RESERVATION.**
*(See page 61.)*

**6** # Mount Everett

SCENERY: ★ ★ ★ ★ ★
TRAIL CONDITION: ★ ★ ★ ★
CHILDREN: ★ ★ ★ ★
DIFFICULTY: ★ ★
SOLITUDE: ★ ★

APPALACHIAN TRAIL
SOUTH

**THE HIKE UP MOUNT EVERETT IS SHORT AND STEEP.**

**GPS TRAILHEAD COORDINATES:** N42° 6.381' W73° 26.070'

**DISTANCE & CONFIGURATION:** 1.5-mile out-and-back

**HIKING TIME:** 1.25 hours

**HIGHLIGHTS:** Panoramic views from summit

**ELEVATION:** 2,602' at summit, 1,760' at trailhead

**ACCESS:** Parking at Mount Everett State Reservation

**MAPS:** Appalachian Trail Conservancy *MA–CT Map 3* and DeLorme *MA Atlas & Gazetteer Map 43*

**CONTACT:** Massachusetts Department of Conservation and Recreation: **mass.gov/eea/agencies/dcr**

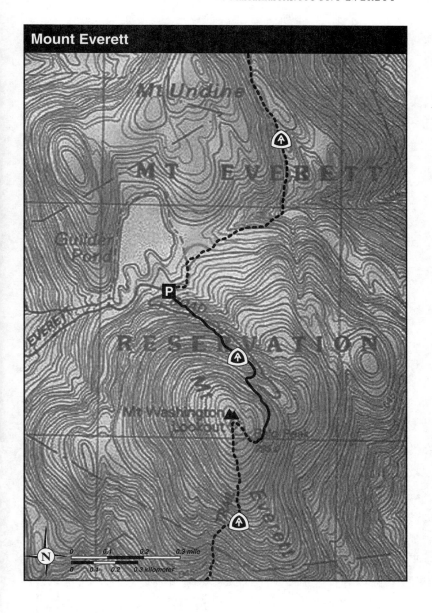

**Mount Everett**

## Overview

Mount Everett is a short hike but impressively steep in some places. Also impressive is the sweeping view of the surrounding backcountry from the top.

## Route Details

The Mount Everett trailhead is distant and remote, being about as far west in western Massachusetts as you can go before you're actually in eastern New York. It's within the Mount Washington State Forest. Follow the road all the way out and around to the Mount Everett State Reservation sign. Follow the road up to the parking area, at which there's plenty of parking for 15 cars or so. There's also an out-house there if you need it before or after your hike. This is also where you can access the Mount Everett auto road when it's open.

The Mount Everett trail, heading southbound on the Appala-chian Trail (A.T.), starts quite steeply right off the bat. You're imme-diately into a steep, sustained climb over a fairly rocky surface. The trail is quite well marked and well-defined. After just a few minutes into the hike, you'll cross over the Mount Everett auto road. Step out onto the auto road, hike up for about 100 feet, and the A.T. will reenter the woods there.

Once the A.T. heads back into the woods, it continues the sus-tained, fairly steep, and rocky ascent. The trail is still well-defined and well marked. Despite its remote location, this is a relatively

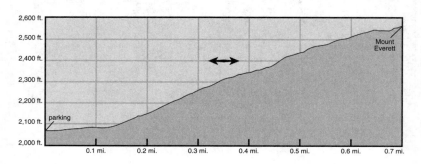

popular hiking destination, given the views that await you at the summit.

About 15 minutes into the hike, the trail heads slightly to the right and gets considerably steeper and rockier. Here you're passing through a short, loosely spaced forest of mostly maple. The forest is quite open and lets in lots of light and lots of breezes. There is also a fairly dense ground cover of ferns. At this point, the A.T. parallels the auto road.

Nearing the summit, the trail veers to the right and again grows steeper and rockier. After about 20 minutes, the trail brings you beneath a large rock ledge of moss-covered granite, which is quite a dramatic sight. There's almost a junglelike quality with the mossy rocks and dense fern ground cover. As you approach that massive rock ledge, the trail switches back sharply to the left and takes you beneath the ledge.

The trail continues its steep and rocky approach to the summit of Mount Everett. You climb up through the rock ledges and emerge at the top at about the 25-minute mark. Atop the rock ledges, the trail is wider but still quite steep and rocky. Now you are also starting to see sweeping views of the woods and mountains to the left (northeast) through the increasingly loosely spaced forest. The trail pitch here is more gradual but the surface no less uneven.

Up here just below the summit, the woods and ground cover are much shorter and scrubbier. The windswept summit cap of Mount Everett feels higher than it might otherwise. Given its isolated location, it would bear the brunt of any weather system coming from any direction.

When you emerge from the trail, you're treated to sweeping 360-degree views of the surrounding mountains and forest, even the Taconic Range in New York to the west. You'll also see the four-posted foundation of the old fire tire that once stood atop Mount Everett from 1915 to 2002. A signpost proclaims the summit elevation at 2,602 feet.

## Nearby Attractions

Great Barrington, Massachusetts, an officially designated Appalachian Trail Community, isn't far and has plenty of lodging and dining options. The rest of Mount Everett State Reservation and nearby Mount Washington State Forest have numerous hiking trails.

## Directions

From US 7 in Great Barrington, Massachusetts, turn onto MA 23 West/MA 41 South and continue 4 miles to South Egremont, Massachusetts. Turn left onto MA 41 South, and then take an immediate right onto Mount Washington Road. Continue for 7.4 miles (this road becomes East Street) to the Mount Everett State Reservation sign on the left; turn left onto Mount Everett Road, and reach the trailhead parking in about 1 mile.

# 7

# Jug End
# State Reservation

SCENERY: ★ ★ ★ ★ ★
TRAIL CONDITION: ★ ★ ★
CHILDREN: ★ ★
DIFFICULTY: ★ ★ ★ ★
SOLITUDE: ★ ★ ★

**SPECTACULAR VIEWS FROM THE TOP OF THE RIDGELINE AT JUG END STATE RESERVATION**

**GPS TRAILHEAD COORDINATES:** N42° 8.668' W73° 25.889'

**DISTANCE & CONFIGURATION:** 8.2-mile out-and-back

**HIKING TIME:** 3.5 hours

**HIGHLIGHTS:** Superb views from atop ridgeline

**ELEVATION:** 1,821' at summit, 350' at trailhead

**ACCESS:** Parking along Jug End Road (a dirt road) at trailhead

**MAPS:** Appalachian Trail Conservancy *MA–CT Map 3* and DeLorme *MA Atlas & Gazetteer Map 43*

**CONTACT:** Massachusetts Department of Conservation and Recreation:
**mass.gov/eea/agencies/dcr**

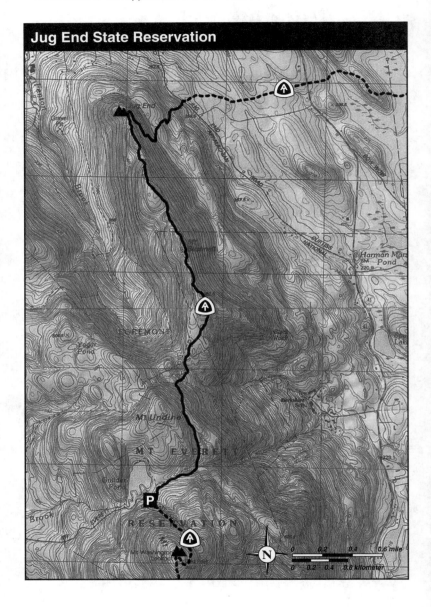

Jug End State Reservation

## Overview

Jug End State Reservation is a long ridgeline hike with impressive views of the mountains and forests of western Massachusetts.

## Route Details

There's a remote feel to the trailhead for Jug End State Reservation and Mount Bushnell. You follow a dirt road down to a small parking area on the right, where there's probably room for four or five cars. The Appalachian Trail (A.T.) climbs sharply up from the dirt road into a dense forest. This first section is a brisk climb—a good, quick, intense warm-up.

After the initial steep climb, the trail mellows slightly, twisting and winding its way through the dense forest. The undulating trail has a root- and rock-strewn surface. It's still steadily climbing here, but it's not as steep as the initial pitch. Deep woods can be quite buggy most of the year, so don't forget your favorite bug stuff.

After about 20 minutes into the hike, the trail pitch mellows considerably. You're hiking along the side of a ridgeline. There are still a couple of short, steep pitches, though. The trail surface is still quite rocky and root-bound, so watch your footing in here. The trail starts switching back and forth up the side of the ridgeline, still a relatively gentle ascent. The forest is still a lush, dense, mixed forest of conifers and hardwoods.

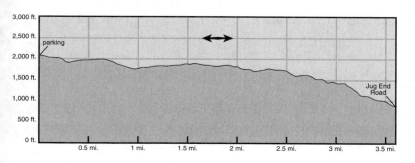

A bit farther in, you'll come to another steep climb up a rocky ledge. This rocky section switches back and forth dramatically as it climbs and is quite strenuous. Watch your step, as a slip here would have unfortunate consequences. Also keep an eye on the white blazes, as it would be fairly easy to follow the rocks and get off trail here.

The trail continues its steep ascent up the side of Mount Bushnell, making a series of switchbacks. There is even a bit of hand-over-hand scrambling in some sections here. The relentless climb continues as you rapidly gain altitude climbing toward the top of the ridgeline. Eventually, you can see the forest canopy becoming thinner, and views of the surrounding hillsides emerge from the distance. Don't take your eye off the ball just yet, though. Watch your footing, stay on the trail, and continue your ascent.

The trail pitch does relax briefly and gets slightly less rocky, but you can tell you're not done with the switchbacks. There are a couple more spots where you're faced with some hand-over-hand scrambling to get up and around the granite chunks. It will soon all be worthwhile.

Toward the end of one of the final switchbacks, you come to a sweeping open view. This is a great place to stop for a while and recharge after your taxing climb up the side of Mount Bushnell. The view from the ridge is spectacular. At this point, you're about 1 hour into the hike. After that ledge with the view, there's one more area of hand-over-hand climbing to get to the true top of the ridgeline.

The trail along the top of the ridgeline of Mount Bushnell passes through a shorter but still fairly dense forest of mostly maple and birch. As always, if you haven't seen a white blaze in a while, simply turn around. There may be one marking the trail in the other direction. The trail continues to roll up and down through the woods atop the ridge, a nice rest after that grueling series of rocky switchbacks. There are still a couple of short, steep pitches, both going up and down, on the ridge. There are also a couple of rock outcrops, making for a dramatic view of the western-Massachusetts forests and hillsides.

The ridge hike is great fun. You've earned it after ascending the side of Mount Bushnell. The trail winds through the forest, with a few hand-over-hand scrambles in some spots. A bit less than 2 hours into your hike, you'll come to an intersection with the blue-blazed Elbow Trail. From this juncture, it's 1.5 miles down to MA 41. The A.T. goes off to the right, heading toward Mount Everett. The hike continues to take you through dense forest toward the two shelter sites.

Eventually, after winding up and down and through the forest, the trail intersects with the Guilder Pond Trail. At this point, you're almost to the Everett Mountain State Reservation parking area. You could combine the Jug End and Mount Everett hikes for an exceptionally long day hike, or turn back here.

## Nearby Attractions

Great Barrington, Massachusetts, isn't far and has plenty of lodging and dining options. The rest of Mount Everett State Reservation and nearby Mount Washington State Forest have numerous hiking trails.

## Directions

From US 7 in Great Barrington, Massachusetts, turn onto MA 23 West/MA 41 South and continue 4 miles to South Egremont, Massachusetts. Turn left onto MA 41 South, and then take an immediate right onto Mount Washington Road. In 0.8 mile, turn left onto The Avenue, which becomes Jug End Road, and follow it 1 mile to the trailhead.

# 8

# East Mountain

SCENERY: ★ ★ ★ ★
TRAIL CONDITION: ★ ★
CHILDREN: ★ ★ ★
DIFFICULTY: ★ ★ ★
SOLITUDE: ★ ★ ★ ★

**EAST MOUNTAIN HAS A BIT OF EVERYTHING, FROM STEEP ROCKY LEDGES TO GENTLE RAMBLES.**

**GPS TRAILHEAD COORDINATES:** N42° 9.288' W73° 20.478'

**DISTANCE & CONFIGURATION:** 2.8-mile out-and-back

**HIKING TIME:** 3 hours

**HIGHLIGHTS:** Impressive views from top of ridgeline

**ELEVATION:** 776' at summit, 65' at trailhead

**ACCESS:** Limited roadside parking

**MAPS:** Appalachian Trail Conservancy *MA–CT Maps 2 and 3* and DeLorme *MA Atlas & Gazetteer Map 44*

**CONTACT:** Massachusetts Department of Conservation and Recreation: **mass.gov/eea/agencies/dcr**

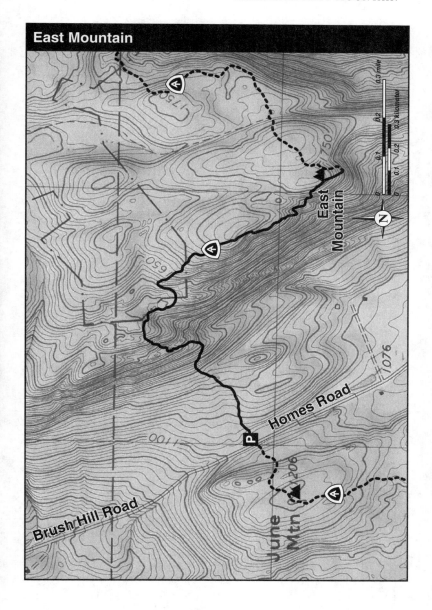

East Mountain

## Overview

East Mountain may be a little hard to find, but once you do, you'll be glad you did. This is classic New England hiking at its finest. The short and steep ascent rewards you with dramatic views of the hillsides to the north and west.

## Route Details

The trail up and around the "summit" of East Mountain seems to skirt around the actual summit. Many of the shorter hikes in southwestern New England are like this. These are classic New England traprock mountain ridges. The middle portion of the hike is indeed quite steep, but the hill and mountaintops have been rounded off by the glaciers long ago. While there is not a summit as defined as that of New England's renowned peaks like Mount Washington or Katahdin, it's still an enjoyable hike and a great way to spend a day. You'll know you've done something after hiking up and down East Mountain.

East Mountain is off to the northeastern side of Brush Hill Road. The Appalachian Trail on the other side of the road leads around June Mountain. The trail itself starts off at a fairly gentle grade right from the road. Keep an eye open for the white blazes. Paying attention to these is the best—if not the only—way to ensure you are indeed on the Appalachian Trail. The trail continues its initial gentle grade, meandering up through a relatively loosely spaced forest. It

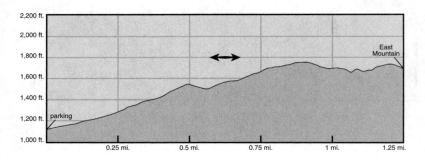

passes within view of a couple of neighboring houses' backyards, but soon you'll be deep in the woods.

After the initial gentle grade, the trail takes on a fairly moderate pitch. It will get your heart pumping, that's for sure, but it's not too bad. This trail would be suitable for hiking with slightly older kids—probably at least 10 or 12 years old. As you get closer to the ridgeline, the pitch of the trail steepens considerably and the trail surface becomes rockier. You're essentially climbing along the side of a ridge. You pass through giant moss-covered rocks protruding from the hillside.

The trail gets quite steep and rocky about 15 or 20 minutes into the hike. There's a nice stone staircase as the trail follows along beneath a large rock ledge. After passing up this stone staircase, you'll be high enough above the forest below that you'll begin to see views of the hillsides to the west.

The trail continues its steep and seemingly unrelenting ascent—switching back through an interesting rock garden. The trail then passes alongside a dramatic rock cliff. The huge granite monoliths make for an impressive display of what the retreating glaciers left us. As the trail veers to the right, you'll see the word *Stop* painted on a downed tree. This is a good alert to keep you on the trail. It would be easy to go straight here and miss it and end up leaving the Appalachian Trail.

The trail dips down into a rocky gorge, then rises sharply again. The trail follows along a very steep ridgeline. The trail itself is quite steep here in this section. There are lots of stone steps and trees to grab on to as the trail passes up and over these massive granite outcrops. Again, it would be easy to lose the trail here, so keep an eye out for the white blazes.

There are dramatic views from the ledge to the north and west through the trees, since you've gained a fair amount of altitude already at this point in the hike. After taking in the views from atop this rock ledge, the trail gives you a bit of a break. The pitch mellows slightly as the trail rolls up and down through the woods and large boulders.

Then the trail descends briefly into a small gulch or ravine. The trail switches back to the right as it drops into this ravine. Here you can begin to hear a stream flowing by somewhere below. When the trail passes over the stream, there's a solidly built wooden footbridge to provide passage between the rock ledges on either side of the stream. After you pass over the footbridge, the trail drops down to the right, then sure enough begins to pitch up once again to another short stone staircase.

Here the trail follows along the top of a moss-covered granite ridgeline, again with dramatic views through the trees of the hillsides and country to the north and west. Don't get too distracted by the views here. The trail then veers to the left. Keep an eye on the white blazes, as this is another spot where it would be fairly easy to keep wandering straight and consequently off the trail.

After this near miss, the trail zigs and zags over moderate terrain at a moderate pitch. Then the trail begins to steepen once again. Here, where the trail is steeper, the trail surface is covered with roots and rocks, so watch your footing. The trail is much more well-defined here, though, and easier to follow.

After traveling up the hillside a bit more, you'll encounter another stone staircase. You'll find that these are often placed in just the right spot to help you up an otherwise steep and unstable section of the trail. The trail is a bit more moderate here after that stone staircase, as it winds its way through a slightly more dense forest than before.

As the trail pitch becomes easier, you'll know you are nearing the summit. The hike finishes not at a dramatic, defined summit per se, but when the trail begins to pitch down, you'll be able to tell you've reached the top of East Mountain. There's a fairly large boulder off to the right of the trail that's also a good indicator of the top.

By all means, though, hike a bit farther to a rock outcrop on the right (northern) side of the trail. The views here to the north and west are indeed dramatic and worth the extra, short walk past the top. This would make for a great place to rest, have a bit of lunch, or take some pictures before turning around and heading back down.

If you do indeed want to hike farther along on the Appalachian Trail, just past the incredible views from the ridgeline, the trail dips dramatically into a good-size rocky gorge. While a few more blazes on the trees would help keep you assured you are on the trail, the trail through this rocky gorge is moderately well-defined.

One of the greatest challenges to hiking East Mountain is quite possibly simply finding the trailhead. There's a small parking spot on the east side of the road (left heading away from Great Barrington) where the Appalachian Trail crosses the road. Parking is limited to two or three vehicles. Plus, the trailheads are not particularly obvious from the road.

Most important, the road leading off US 7 wasn't marked as indicated on maps. It's supposed to be Brush Hill Road, which turns into Homes Road. Farther down, it is indeed marked that way. Right off US 7 heading into Great Barrington, though, the road that becomes Brush Hill is marked as Brookside. Keep that in mind when you're looking for the trailhead. Nevertheless, once you do find it, it's well worth the hike.

## Nearby Attractions

Great Barrington and Stockbridge, Massachusetts, are nearby, with numerous lodging and dining options. Tanglewood Music Center has a fairly extensive concert schedule during the summer.

## Directions

Following US 7 North into Great Barrington, Massachusetts, you'll see Brookside Road on the right before you get into the downtown area. On many maps (including the Appalachian Trail Conservancy maps), it's marked as Brush Hill Road. Turn right onto Brookside, which is later marked as Brush Hill. Follow this road 2 miles until you come to the small, roadside dirt parking area on the left. If the road turns to Home Road or you enter the town of Sheffield, you've gone too far.

# 9

# Benedict Pond and The Ledges

THE LEDGES HIKE TAKES YOU UP AND ACROSS IMPRESSIVELY
STEEP ROCK LEDGES.

**GPS TRAILHEAD COORDINATES:** N42° 12.169' W73° 17.321'

**DISTANCE & CONFIGURATION:** 3-mile out-and-back

**HIKING TIME:** 1.5 hours

**HIGHLIGHTS:** Dramatic views of Benedict Pond and the rest of Beartown State Forest

**ELEVATION:** 1,863' at summit, 1,580' at trailhead

**ACCESS:** Benedict Pond parking area ($5 fee)

**MAPS:** Appalachian Trail Conservancy MA–CT Map 2 and DeLorme MA Atlas & Gazetteer Map 44

**CONTACT:** Massachusetts Department of Conservation and Recreation: **mass.gov/eea/agencies/dcr**

## Benedict Pond and The Ledges

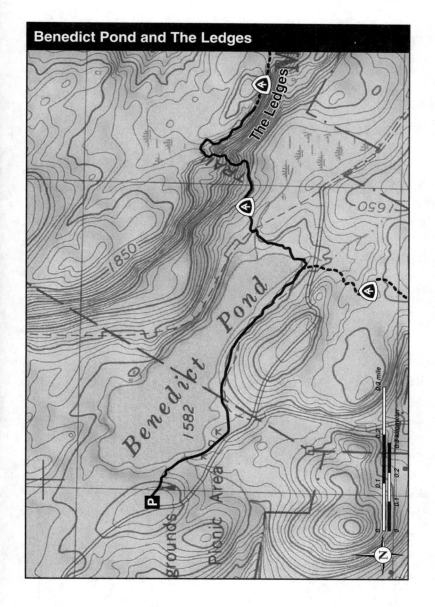

## Overview

The views of Benedict Pond as you're hiking in and the views of the surrounding forest from the top of The Ledges make this a spectacular hike.

## Route Details

There are tons of hiking trails throughout Beartown State Forest. To hike up to The Ledges, you'll start out on the blue-blazed Benedict Pond Trail heading toward the intersection with the Appalachian Trail (A.T.). The Benedict Pond loop leading to the A.T. is a mostly flat, rocky trail that meanders around the pond. You could take a dip in Benedict Pond after your hike on a hot summer's day. There are plenty of spots to stop and just sit by the pond as well.

After about 10 minutes in on the Benedict Pond loop, you'll come to the first intersection with the Appalachian Trail heading south. The southbound A.T. heads off to the right. Continue northbound on the trail to The Ledges Trail. Now you're following both white and blue blazes.

There are a lot of open spots and views of the pond on this part of the trail. You'll also have plenty of company, as this is quite a popular trail. After the trail passes over a large bridge over a stream feeding into Benedict Pond, you'll come to the point at which the A.T. and the Benedict Pond loop split. Follow the signs for the A.T.

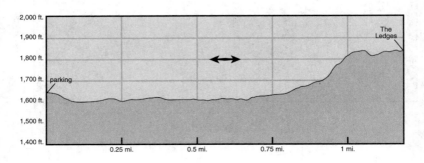

and The Ledges trail off to the right (north). After the split, the trail pitches up quite a bit, but this is still a good kid-friendly hike.

The trail here is quite well-defined as it passes through a forest of medium-height, lush, green maple trees. About 20 minutes into the hike, the trail veers sharply to the left, past the first of many rock ledges you'll encounter. The trail follows along the bottom of the ledge. The trail gets considerably steeper and rockier here. A set of stone steps helps you along the way toward the top of the first rock ledge. The trail continues its steep and rocky ascent, switching back and forth upward past other smaller rock ledges.

The trail continues up through interesting rock gardens and smaller ledges toward a massive rock ledge that starts to emerge through the forest. Continue up another set of stone steps. You're definitely gaining some altitude here. That massive rock ledge is across a deep gulch, making for a very dramatic sight.

After reaching the same height as the top of that rock ledge across from you, the trail mellows somewhat. You cross over a small footbridge over a stream that runs down into and through the gulch. The trail also splits here, so go right over the bridge to stay on the A.T.

After you cross over the footbridge, climb straight up and over the rocks to stay on the A.T. The trail gets a little marshy and rocky here, then heads right and traverses along the top of the massive rock ledge you've been seeing from across the gulch. The trail is fairly rocky and does a lot of up and down here. Watch your step, as a fall here would really not be good.

Following along the top of the rock ledge (after all, the trail is called The Ledges) is quite dramatic. Soon, you'll come to a clearing in the trees on the right where you can sit and look out over Beartown State Forest. There's one primary clearing and a couple of other smaller ones just past that. You'll know the epic open ledge when you come to it. The open ledge and views from here are impressive.

## Nearby Attractions

Great Barrington and Stockbridge, Massachusetts, are nearby, with numerous lodging and dining options. Tanglewood Music Center has a fairly extensive concert schedule during the summer.

## Directions

From US 7 in Great Barrington, Massachusetts, follow MA 23 East/ MA 183 South 3.5 miles, and then continue another 1.8 miles on MA 23 to Blue Hill Road. Turn left and follow Blue Hill Road 2.2 miles to a right turn for Beartown State Forest. Follow the access road 0.5 mile to Benedict Pond parking.

**10** # Cobble Hill
## (also called Tyringham Cobble)

SCENERY: ★ ★ ★
TRAIL CONDITION: ★ ★ ★ ★
CHILDREN: ★ ★ ★ ★
DIFFICULTY: ★ ★ ★
SOLITUDE: ★ ★ ★ ★

**THE VIEW FROM ATOP COBBLE HILL REVEALS THE VERDANT LANDSCAPE BELOW.**

**GPS TRAILHEAD COORDINATES:** N42° 14.087' W73° 11.653'

**DISTANCE & CONFIGURATION:** 4-mile out-and-back

**HIKING TIME:** 2 hours

**HIGHLIGHTS:** Fantastic views atop Cobble Hill

**ELEVATION:** 1,358' at summit, 900' at trailhead

**ACCESS:** Unrestricted, established parking spot for approximately eight vehicles

**MAPS:** Appalachian Trail Conservancy *MA–CT Map 2* and DeLorme *MA Atlas & Gazetteer Map 44*

**CONTACT:** Massachusetts Department of Conservation and Recreation:
**mass.gov/eea/agencies/dcr**

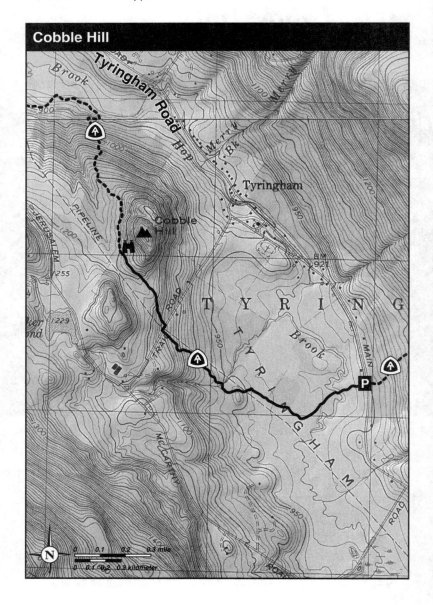

Cobble Hill

## Overview

The hike up to Cobble Hill is multifaceted and has plenty of flexible options for bringing along hikers of all shapes and sizes and ages. Going all the way up to the top of Cobble Hill is well worth it for the dramatic views of the lush valley below.

## Route Details

Like most of the Appalachian Trail as it passes through New England, there are trailheads on either side of the road where the trail crosses. From the established parking area, the trailhead for Cobble Hill is to the west (the right side of the road heading away from the highway) and the Baldy Mountain trailhead is to the east (the left side of the road).

The trail starts off as a grass-covered trail leading you through a lush grove of dense undergrowth. It's also a fairly swampy area, so you'll soon encounter a series of footbridges, some of which are quite long and extensive. The trail starts out and continues for quite some time meandering through the fields and into the woods.

From the trailhead on Tyringham Road, it's 1.1 miles to Jerusalem Road, another spot nearby where you can pick up the trail. From the trailhead on Tyringham Road, it's also 7 miles to the Mount Wilcox shelter in Beartown State Forest if you wanted to piece together a brief section hike. As always, these distances are marked on the wooden Appalachian Trail signs posted at fairly regular intervals.

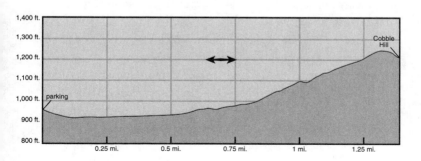

The gentle nature of most of this hike and the multiple out-and-back options make this a good kid-friendly hike. Little kids will also delight in walking along the wooden walkways constructed over the marshy areas at the beginning of the hike. You could hike over and through the marsh, over the field and into the woods, then turn around when you get to the streambed. Or you could continue to the edge of the farmer's field. Or, if you wanted to get right to the climb up Cobble Hill, you could start the hike where the trail crosses over Jerusalem Road. It all depends on your energy level and that of your hiking companions.

Just after starting off on the grassy trail, you come to the first of an extensive series of footbridges and ramps. These take you over what would be a virtually impassable swampy area. The wooden ramp winds through the marshy area and over a small river, then deposits you at the edge of a large open field. Looking across the field ahead and to the north, you can see Cobble Hill. Traversing this marsh could be quite buggy at the right time of year and time of day, so don't forget your favorite bug repellent.

At the edge of the field, the trail takes you along the southern border of the field. This is quite a relaxing hike. Following along the edge of the field, there are a couple more wooden ramps and platforms that take you over some muddy, eroded areas. When you encounter these, please use them. They are put there to help prevent further erosion and to maintain the existing character of the land surrounding the trail. So even though they might seem a bit weak and wobbly, step lightly and carefully, and please use any established ramps or footbridges.

After hiking for a couple hundred feet along the edge of the field, the trail then reenters the woods. There is another series of footbridges here, as the ground surface is quite muddy. The footbridges here are much sturdier—the classic Appalachian Trail footbridges with thick 10-foot-long beams supported on either end. They look like something kids would build out of Lincoln Logs.

Deeper into the woods, the trail surface is covered with lots of roots and a dense bed of pine needles. Here the trail still follows the border of the open field and the forest. It's still quite flat even this far from the Tyringham Road trailhead. The trail pops out into the open once more before diving back into the woods. Here it also crosses through a fence that looks like it was intended to keep cattle from roaming. After getting through the gate, the trail hits the woods and begins a gentle ascent.

The character of the forest is a shimmering green, as it's composed primarily of tall older white pines and younger gray birch. While you have a gained a bit of altitude, the trail is still mostly a gentle ramble through the woods. Again, this makes this part of the hike exceptionally kid friendly. The trail passes over what looks like an old fire road bed and a couple more of the Appalachian Trail footbridges. Then you come to a bridge over a stream. This is one possible place to turn around if you have very young kids hiking with you. At the very least, they will likely want to stop and play in the stream.

After crossing over the stream, the trail continues its ramble through the woods. There will be another series of footbridges along the way as well. Watch your step on these, as they can be somewhat slick when they're wet. After passing over a series of these footbridges, the trail pitches up and veers to the right (north-northwest) and comes to the border of a fairly steep hillside field encircled by a barbed wire cow fence. There is a step contraption built out of wood that you can use to climb over the barbed wire. Be extremely careful here. It works, but it would be fairly easy to take a tumble here as well.

After you've crossed over this funky little step, follow the trail as it cuts directly across the field. On the far side of the field, you have another wooden step up and over the barbed wire fence. Again, be very careful during this process. Once you've crossed over and out of the field, you're on Jerusalem Road. There isn't much parking here, but there's certainly room for a few cars on the side of the road. This is another start-stop option if you only wanted to climb Cobble Hill.

From where the trail meets the road, walk downhill to the right about 50 feet and pick up the trail where it reenters the woods.

At this point, you've come 1.1 miles from the Tyringham Road trailhead. Here's where the trail begins ascending in earnest. The Cobble Hill Trail is beautifully well maintained and established. As soon as you enter the woods, you begin a moderate yet steady climb through the forest of massive white pines.

The trail intersects with the Cobble Loop Trail, marked with blue blazes. So for this section, you'll be following both the white blazes of the Appalachian Trail and the blue blazes of the Cobble Loop Trail. The trail continues its steady ascent. The trail surface is mostly smooth, hard-packed ground, so the hiking is relatively easy.

The trail takes you in and out of the woods, and eventually to a short, steep cliff with some hand-over-hand scrambling. You're almost at the top at this point. After the cliff, the trail grade becomes more moderate and the trail veers around to the left (north). Keep an eye to the right and you'll come to an open rock outcrop with a dramatic view of the valley below.

## Nearby Attractions

There's the trailhead for Baldy Mountain right across the street if you didn't get enough hiking on the Cobble Hill Trail. The towns of Stockbridge and Great Barrington, Massachusetts, are nearby, and Tanglewood Music Center is close and hosts a series of concerts throughout the summer.

## Directions

From Exit 2 off I-90 (the Massachusetts Turnpike) in Lee, Massachusetts, follow MA 102 toward Great Barrington, Massachusetts. Just after turning onto MA 102, turn left onto Tyringham Road (across from the Big Y store). Follow this road through Tyringham. Parking for the trailhead will be on the right (north) about 1 mile past the center of Tyringham, 5 miles from MA 102.

# 11

# Baldy Mountain

SCENERY: ★ ★
TRAIL CONDITION: ★ ★ ★
CHILDREN: ★ ★ ★
DIFFICULTY: ★ ★ ★
SOLITUDE: ★ ★ ★ ★

**FARMLAND ONCE COVERED THIS AREA, AS INDICATED BY AN OLD STONE WALL.**

**GPS TRAILHEAD COORDINATES:** N42° 14.087' W73° 11.653'

**DISTANCE & CONFIGURATION:** 3.2-mile out-and-back

**HIKING TIME:** 1.75 hours

**HIGHLIGHTS:** Open, scenic forest

**ELEVATION:** 1,873' at summit, 900' at trailhead

**ACCESS:** Unrestricted, established parking spot for approximately eight vehicles

**MAPS:** Appalachian Trail Conservancy *MA–CT Map 2* and DeLorme *MA Atlas & Gazetteer Map 44*

**CONTACT:** Massachusetts Department of Conservation and Recreation:
**mass.gov/eea/agencies/dcr**

## Baldy Mountain

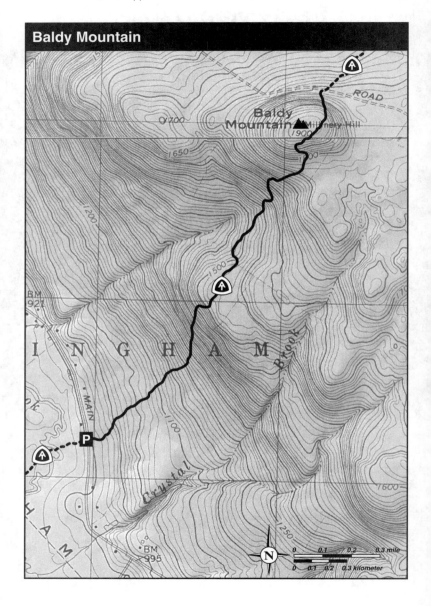

## Overview

Baldy Mountain is a nice, relaxing, and scenic hike, but there's not much of a defined summit. You really only realize you've reached the top when you start going down on the other side.

## Route Details

There's no real peak or outcrop with a view of any sort atop Baldy Mountain, but it's still a nice ramble through the forest. You park in the same spot as the Cobble Hill trailhead. The Baldy Mountain trailhead is on the other side of the road.

The trail starts off flat and stays at a moderate grade for quite a distance. It winds through the mossy forest with towering trees forming the forest canopy. The relative lack of undergrowth gives the forest an open feel. The trail passes over a gentle stream and then becomes slightly steeper. The trail also passes over an old stone wall—evidence of the farmland that once covered most of the area. You hear the sound of the stream rushing by as you follow along and then cross over the old wall of moss-covered stones.

After crossing the wall, the trail pitches up slightly but still holds a fairly moderate grade. The forest is still very open at the floor level— minimal undergrowth. The trail is well marked with white blazes.

The trail maintains a steady but moderate pitch through the open forest. After 30 minutes or so, the trail veers to the right and the pitch increases slightly. The forest is still quite open here but

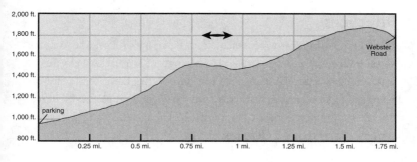

starting to fill in a bit more with undergrowth. The forest also starts to become more coniferous than deciduous. As the trail pitches up, the trail surface also starts to get a bit rockier.

There's more of a shaded feel as the trail starts to switch back and forth up the steeper hillside. Now you're walking beneath a forest canopy of tall conifers. The trail is definitely steeper here. It's still not excessive, but it will get the heart pumping. In this section where the trail is steeper and rockier, there is still an abundant number of white blazes, so following the trail is easy.

After a good, sustained elevation gain, the trail veers again to the right and mellows slightly. You are almost to the top at this point. The summit, such as it is, is a fairly flat plateau surrounded by fairly dense forest. There's not a clear, truly defined summit. You'll know you've arrived as you start to descend on the far side. So there's not much of a view of the surrounding hillsides and forest, but the view of the forest surrounding you is quite pleasant in and of itself. If you just planned to hike Baldy Mountain, stop or turn around as you begin a gentle descent—or you just may end up in Georgia.

## Nearby Attractions

The trailhead for Cobble Hill is right across the street, if you didn't get enough hiking on the Baldy Mountain Trail. The towns of Stockbridge and Great Barrington, Massachusetts, are nearby, and Tanglewood Music Center is close and hosts a series of concerts throughout the summer.

## Directions

From Exit 2 off I-90 (the Massachusetts Turnpike) in Lee, Massachusetts, follow MA 102 toward Great Barrington, Massachusetts. Just after turning onto MA 102, turn left onto Tyringham Road (across from the Big Y store). Follow this road through Tyringham. Parking for the trailhead will be on the right (north) about 1 mile past the center of Tyringham, 5 miles from MA 102.

# 12

# Becket Mountain

SCENERY: ★ ★ ★ ★
TRAIL CONDITION: ★ ★ ★
CHILDREN: ★ ★ ★
DIFFICULTY: ★ ★ ★
SOLITUDE: ★ ★ ★

**BECKET MOUNTAIN TRAIL OFFERS AN IDEAL SPOT FOR LUNCH AT THE SUMMIT.**

**GPS TRAILHEAD COORDINATES:** N42° 17.423' W73° 9.335'

**DISTANCE & CONFIGURATION:** 3.2-mile out-and-back

**HIKING TIME:** 2.25 hours

**HIGHLIGHTS:** Peaceful grove at summit

**ELEVATION:** 2,178' at summit, 1,400' at trailhead

**ACCESS:** Parking area off US 20

**MAPS:** Appalachian Trail Conservancy *MA–CT Map 2* and DeLorme *MA Atlas & Gazetteer Map 32*

**CONTACT:** Massachusetts Department of Conservation and Recreation: **mass.gov/eea/agencies/dcr**

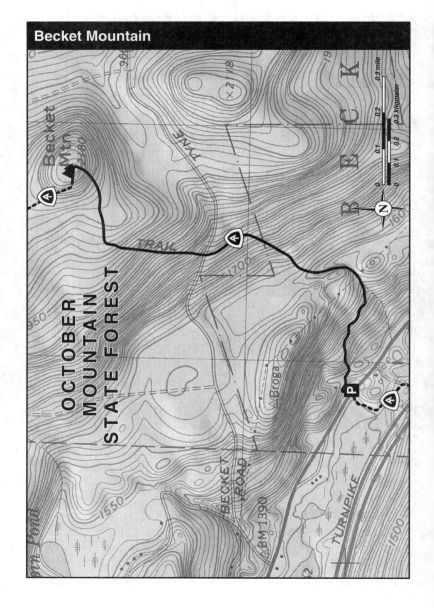

## Overview

Becket Mountain is a nice, long hike but quite gentle and scenic.

## Route Details

The trailhead for Becket Mountain is just north of where the large Appalachian Trail (A.T.) bridge crosses over I-90. Take a short walk up US 20 to get to the actual trailhead from the parking area. Walking along the guardrail, you'll know you're there when you get to a staircase leading up to US 20 and signs for the A.T. A small cairn marks the trailhead.

As soon as you enter the woods, the trail ascends steeply. It is well marked and well-defined at this initial section. After 75 feet or so, the trail splits. There is a blue-blazed trail to the left, and the white-blazed A.T. heads off to the right. After the split, the trail's pitch mellows and the trail crosses a small stream. There's an A.T. signpost here stating the distances to the October Mountain and Kay Woods shelters at 7.2 and 16 miles, respectively.

The trail pitches up more steeply after passing the A.T. signpost. There's a stone staircase that helps you up the steepest chunk. The surrounding forest becomes denser here as well. Here you lose sight of US 20, and your hike becomes a bit quieter as you get farther from the road. The trail is still well marked here, but heed the white blazes as you traverse a rock garden where it would be easy to

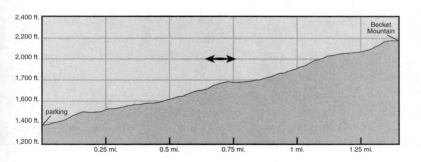

wander off-trail. After another short, steep section, the trail flattens out and passes through a corridor of baby conifers.

The trail crosses over a private blue-blazed trail, then continues north, following the course of a stream running through a deep gully. Where the trails are muddy in places like this, be sure to walk on the wooden footbridges or on rocks to prevent trail erosion. The A.T. continues straight up past the stream on the right. It passes under some power lines, then heads back into the woods. The trail is fairly flat here but, after a stream crossing, begins to get steeper again. Be careful with this stream crossing, as the boulders are often slick, especially the more moss-covered ones.

The A.T. bears toward the left after the stream and continues at a moderate grade, rolling up and down and switching back through the loosely spaced forest. This would certainly make a nice hike with kids. It's a beautiful hike on a nice, sunny day with lots of light filtering down through the trees. At this part of the hike, you can still hear a bit of rumble from I-90, but that fades as you get farther along. It can be occasionally hard to spot the next blaze, and some have been there for a while, so they may be a bit faded. Just keep a sharp eye out, as always.

The trail continues its moderate ascent, switching back through the open forest. The trail is quite well-defined here as it follows along the ridgeline heading west. Then you'll cross over the paved Tyne Road. This could also be a good alternate parking spot if you have much smaller kids hiking with you, as there is room for a couple of cars to park here along the road.

After crossing over the road, the trail passes by a rocky cliff on the right—a large pile of boulders left there by the retreating glaciers. The trail has a moderate pitch here but a steady uphill rise. The trail surface is fairly rocky, so it can be slick when it's wet. The trail rises slowly and steadily along the ridgeline through a nice, open forest. The only sounds you hear now are the sounds of the forest. The trail is quite well-defined here as well. As it meanders up the mountainside, it flattens out a bit with one final, slightly steeper lunge just before you reach the top.

At the top of Becket Mountain, there's a grove of gray birch. There's an A.T. trail register nailed to a tree with a sign indicating you're in the right place. Just past the top, there's a huge pine tree and a massive boulder that make a good spot to stop for lunch. The summit of Becket Mountain is much more defined than some of the other, lesser drumlins in southwestern New England.

## Nearby Attractions

The towns of Stockbridge and Great Barrington, Massachusetts, are relatively close. Tanglewood Music Center is close and hosts a series of concerts throughout the summer.

## Directions

Take Exit 2 off I-90 (the Massachusetts Turnpike) in Lee, Massachusetts, follow US 20 East 4.7 miles to trailhead parking on the right (south) side of US 20.

**Warner Hill**

| | |
|---|---|
| SCENERY: ★ ★ ★ | |
| TRAIL CONDITION: ★ ★ ★ ★ | |
| CHILDREN: ★ ★ ★ ★ | |
| DIFFICULTY: ★ ★ | |
| SOLITUDE: ★ ★ ★ | |

**WARNER HILL IS A PERFECT FIRST HIKE FOR KIDS.**

**GPS TRAILHEAD COORDINATES:** N42° 24.461' W73° 9.234'

**DISTANCE & CONFIGURATION:** 0.8-mile out-and-back

**HIKING TIME:** 1 hour

**HIGHLIGHTS:** Scenic forest

**ELEVATION:** 2,050' at summit, 1,620' at trailhead

**ACCESS:** Small parking area with room for five or six cars

**MAPS:** Appalachian Trail Conservancy MA–CT Maps 1 and 2 and DeLorme MA Atlas & Gazetteer Map 33

**CONTACT:** Massachusetts Department of Conservation and Recreation: **mass.gov/eea/agencies/dcr**

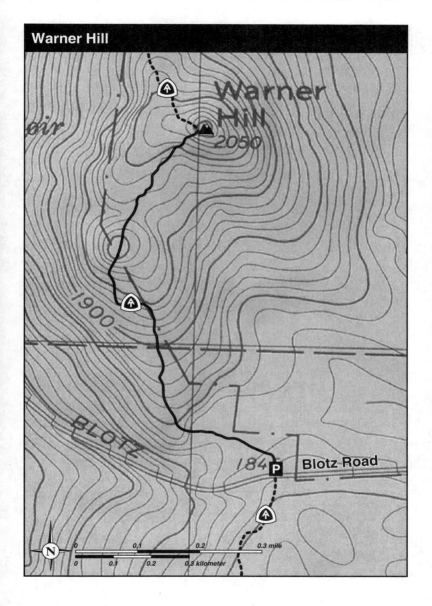

## Overview

Warner Hill is the most kid-friendly hike described in this book. Its gentle grade takes you through a scenic forest.

## Route Details

This is a perfect first hike for small children, as it is safe and very gentle. The trailhead is somewhat remote, but if you're looking for a nice, gentle hike through a spectacularly scenic forest to introduce your progeny to the wonders of a walk in the woods, this is it.

The trail up Warner Hill leads right out from the parking area on Blotz Road. It starts off very well-defined, sloping downward slightly and to the left a bit at first. The trail traverses a swampy area with a couple of wooden Appalachian Trail (A.T.) footbridges. Then the trail meanders at a relatively flat grade through the lush green forest of mostly deciduous trees—maples and birch.

After 10 minutes or so into the hike, the trail veers to the right and begins a gentle ascent. Here the trail surface is quite covered with roots and rocks. There's a beautiful, high-canopy pine forest that lets in lots of light to the forest floor.

The trail pitch takes a gentle rambling ascent up a truly scenic trail and forest. There are still lots of roots and rocks underfoot, so little feet should be careful negotiating their steps. Here the trail again veers to the left and flattens out as it strolls through a lush bed of ferns.

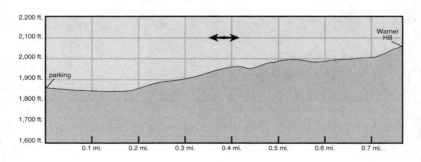

Then the trail starts rolling up and down and continues gently winding its way through the forest. The summit of Warner Hill is one of those summits that's not very well-defined. The summit, such as it is, does not have a clearing with a commanding view or a truly defined peak. There is a tree with a white blaze of the Appalachian Trail with a yellow blaze tucked in right next to it. There's also part of an old stone wall running nearby the top.

Just hiking to the top of Warner Hill makes for a truly kid-friendly hike. Your kids will be energized about the hike, but not wiped out by overexertion. If you're with older kids or other adults, you can make this a much longer hike by continuing on to Tully Mountain and the Kay Wood shelter. The trail begins a steady descent after the yellow- and white-blazed tree and the stone wall, so that's clearly the "summit" of Warner Hill.

If you wanted to continue on the Tully Mountain, you could do a longer out-and-back or leave a car at the Tully Mountain trailhead and do an even longer one-way hike.

The scenic forest and gentle grade of the trail and the overall short duration make it a perfect introduction to hiking. Be sure to bring the bug stuff, though. It could get mighty buggy in the lower swampy sections.

## Nearby Attractions

The city of Pittsfield, Massachusetts, is nearby, with plenty of lodging and dining options. You are also close to October Mountain State Forest, with plenty of hiking, camping, and canoeing.

## Directions

Follow MA 8 South about 6.5 miles out of Pittsfield, Massachusetts, through the town of Hinsdale. Turn right onto Pittsfield Road. In 0.8 mile, this becomes Blotz Road (after the intersection with Plunkett Road). Continue another 1 mile, and trailhead parking will be on the right.

**Tully Mountain**

SCENERY: ★ ★ ★
TRAIL CONDITION: ★ ★ ★
CHILDREN: ★ ★ ★
DIFFICULTY: ★ ★ ★
SOLITUDE: ★ ★ ★

**THE TULLY MOUNTAIN HIKE WINDS THROUGH AN EVER-CHANGING FOREST.**

**GPS TRAILHEAD COORDINATES:** N42° 27.408' W73° 9.738'

**DISTANCE & CONFIGURATION:** 4.2-mile out-and-back

**HIKING TIME:** 3.25 hours

**HIGHLIGHTS:** Dramatic, changing character of forest

**ELEVATION:** 2,080' at summit, 1,385' at trailhead

**ACCESS:** Trailhead parking off road

**MAPS:** Appalachian Trail Conservancy *MA–CT Maps 1 and 2* and DeLorme *MA Atlas & Gazetteer Map 33*

**CONTACT:** Massachusetts Department of Conservation and Recreation: **mass.gov/eea/agencies/dcr**

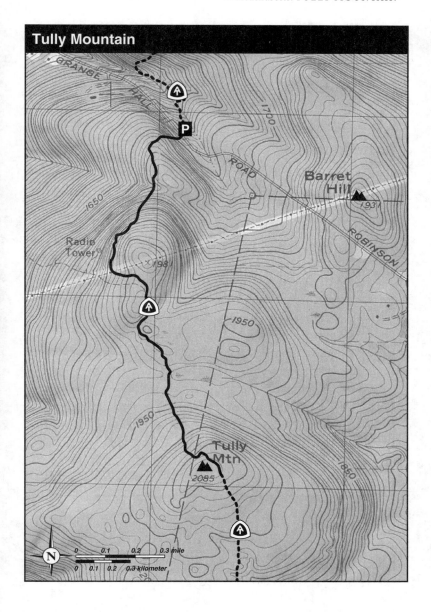

Tully Mountain

## Overview

Tully Mountain is a nice rambling hike through forests and fern beds and side hills and gullies. The trail continues on to Warner Hill, so you could combine this hike with a continued hike to Warner Hill for a longer excursion.

## Route Details

The Tully Mountain Trail starts with a brisk climb right from the road. After that fairly brisk initial climb, the trail mellows out slightly and winds through a fairly dense, mixed deciduous-and-coniferous forest. Then the trail switches back to the left and continues a steady yet gentle ascent. About 15 minutes into the hike, the trail pitch grows mellower still.

Then the trail climbs a short rise and passes an old stone fireplace foundation on the left. Shortly after passing that old fireplace, the trail drops down into and passes through a wide gully. The open hillside faces you as you descend through and across the gully, then begin climbing on the other side. The trail is quite well-defined here, so there's very little risk of wandering off the trail.

The trail continues a steady ascent along a hillside. It's not too steep here but gets a bit more root and rock covered. This is a good kid-friendly hike, though it's a bit steeper and longer than the nearby Warner Hill Trail. There's a set of granite steps leading you up and

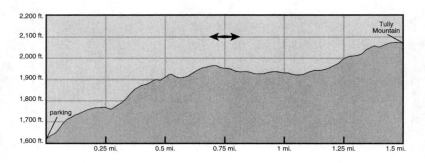

farther along the hillside. The trail remains fairly rocky and actually crosses what looks like the remnants of a rockslide from years ago.

Then you pass through this field within the forest with tall grasses and ferns blanketing the forest floor. It's quite a dramatic sight. The entire rounded hilltop to the left of the Appalachian Trail (A.T.) is covered with this forest field. After that, the trail descends through another small ravine or gully. You'll pass under a set of power lines at about 35 minutes into the hike.

The forest cover is denser here as the trail reenters the forest after passing under the power lines. The trail continues a gentle ascent. The brief, steep climb at the beginning of the hike and the rocky section before the power lines notwithstanding, this is still quite a kid-friendly hike.

Then the trail passes across a lazy little stream. The ground remains a bit muddier here. You'll also encounter a long series of A.T. footbridges. Some are a little wobbly, so watch your step in this section. After passing over those, the trail descends a bit to another set of footbridges. The ground here is still quite swampy and damp. This fairly extensive series of footbridges is quite a distance from trailheads on either side, so you have to admire the effort of the trail crews in building this network of footbridges.

The trail passes through another swampy section and begins a gentle climb toward the top of Tully Mountain and on toward Warner Hill. As the trail continues its gentle ascent around the top plateau of Tully Mountain, it gets slightly rockier. At about 1 hour and 15 minutes into the hike, you'll pass through an open grove of maples with fern ground cover. The trail continues through the loose mixed forest with lots of fern ground cover.

The Tully Mountain hike isn't a dramatic up-and-down summit hike. It's more of a gentle ramble through the woods. The trail gently rolls up and down and winds through the fairly dense mixed forest. The trail continues its gentle rise and fall through the forest. At 1 hour and 20 minutes in, you'll pass a small stream running past a short ledge. It can be slick scrambling up here, so watch your footing.

The trail passes a couple more streams and swampy areas, so don't forget your favorite bug stuff. Mosquitoes love this sort of damp, swampy forest.

At 1 hour and 45 minutes, you come to a slightly more open hilltop, where the forest isn't quite as dense. Looking around here through the trees, you can't see any other points of land higher than where you are here. This is the southeastern portion of the Tully plateau. At the highest point on the plateau, there's a scenic spot to stop and have lunch.

You could turn around here or continue through to Warner Hill. It's 1 hour and 45 minutes to the "summit" table here at Tully. If you continued on the trail here, it would rise and fall gently down the flank of Tully Mountain and up the side of Warner Hill.

## Nearby Attractions

The city of Pittsfield, Massachusetts, is nearby, with plenty of lodging and dining options. You are also close to October Mountain State Forest, with plenty of hiking, camping, and canoeing.

## Directions

From the intersection of US 7 and US 20 in Pittsfield, Massachusetts, follow East Street/MA 9 1.2 miles. Turn right to stay on East Street, and continue another 2.1 miles. Continue straight on South Street for 1 mile, and turn right onto Grange Hill Road. Trailhead parking will be on your left in about 1 mile. Alternatively, from the town of Hinsdale, follow Robinson Road 2.2 miles to the west (it will turn into Grange Hill Road). Trailhead parking is on the right.

# Mount Williams

SCENERY: ★ ★ ★ ★
TRAIL CONDITION: ★ ★ ★ ★
CHILDREN: ★ ★ ★
DIFFICULTY: ★ ★ ★
SOLITUDE: ★ ★ ★ ★

**THE HIKE UP MOUNT WILLIAMS REWARDS YOU WITH SWEEPING VIEWS OF THE WESTERN MASSACHUSETTS BACKCOUNTRY.**

**GPS TRAILHEAD COORDINATES:** N42° 41.246' W73° 9.507'

**DISTANCE & CONFIGURATION:** 1.6-mile out-and-back

**HIKING TIME:** 1.5 hours

**HIGHLIGHTS:** Open ledge with sweeping views at summit

**ELEVATION:** 2,951' at summit, 2,300' at trailhead

**ACCESS:** Trailhead parking off Notch Road (closed late November–early June) or Reservoir Road

**MAPS:** Appalachian Trail Conservancy *MA–CT Map 1* and DeLorme *MA Atlas & Gazetteer Map 21*

**CONTACT:** Massachusetts Department of Conservation and Recreation: **mass.gov/eea/agencies/dcr**

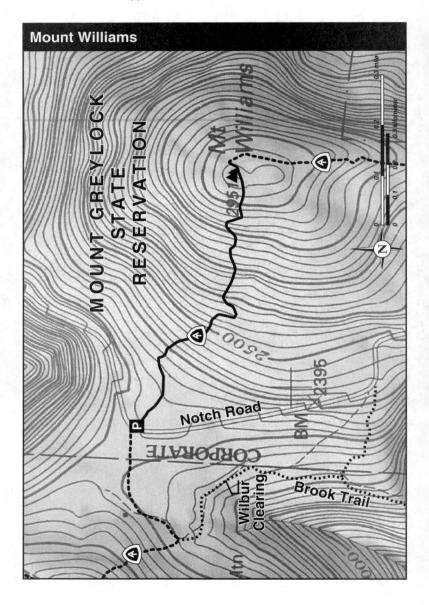

Mount Williams

## Overview

Mount Williams is in the less-traveled part of Mount Greylock State Reservation, so you can find a bit of solitude and some impressive views to the north and east.

## Route Details

There are myriad hiking options within Mount Greylock State Reservation. Mount Williams is a nice medium-length and medium-intensity hike that ends on a ledge with sweeping views of the surrounding forests and hills. The trailhead for Mount Williams is up off the summit road leading to the top of Mount Greylock. Drive past the Notch Gate parking area to the Wilbur's Clearing area, a small parking lot off to the left of the summit road with room for about 10 cars.

From the parking area, follow a blue-blazed trail to where it intersects with the Appalachian Trail (A.T.). This spur trail is well marked and well-defined, with a firm, hard-packed trail surface. You're hiking through a beautiful, dense forest of maple, birch, and pine. Here you can still hear the sound of vehicles driving up the auto road to the summit of Greylock, but it won't be long before you're deep enough into the woods that all you'll hear is the sound track of the forest.

After about 10 minutes on this blue-blazed trail, you'll come to the intersection with Old Summit Road. A ski trail heads to the right. Keep to the left; shortly after that intersection, you'll come to the A.T.

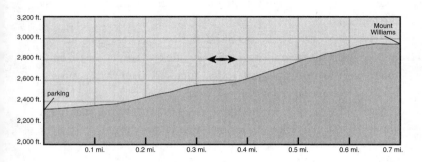

Taking the A.T. to the left is the northbound route. Stay right and follow the A.T. southbound to the summit of Mount Williams. Take a look around at this intersection from the other direction. You won't want to miss this turnoff on the way back. If you do, though, it's no big deal. When you hit the auto road, just turn left and head back up to the Wilbur's Clearing parking area. It just makes the hike a little longer, and you'll have a longer time on the paved road.

Once you're on the southbound A.T. heading up Mount Williams, the trail pitch picks up a bit, but it is still a fairly moderate grade. The trail surface is quite root-bound, and the trail itself takes a serpentine path up the hillside. At about 15 minutes into the hike, the trail veers to the right and the trail pitch steepens. The trail is now taking you on a sustained but still relatively moderate ascent.

Then the trail switches back ever so slightly to the left, and the trail gets a bit steeper. Right after this, you'll come to a stone staircase. The forest here is still quite dense, with a moderately high canopy and dense undergrowth. The trail continues its sustained, moderate ascent and begins to pass through a grove of tall, slender pines, bare down at the forest level from reaching up to the sun above the forest canopy. It makes for a dramatically scenic forest.

As with most of the trails in Mount Greylock State Reservation, this trail is often heavily used, so they're well maintained and well marked. At about 25 minutes into the hike, the trail veers to the left and passes through a root-and-rock-filled small ravine. The trail continues its sustained yet steady climb. There are a few steeper spots here and there, but for the most part it maintains a relatively moderate pitch.

After about 35 minutes of hiking, you'll notice that the trail does get a bit steeper and stays that way. The trail surface is still quite rough with lots of roots and rocks. There are many little culverts leading into or away from the trail. Keep an eye on the white blazes, as it would be easy to misinterpret these culverts as the trail itself. The trail continues with increasingly tighter switchbacks as you get higher on Mount Williams. At the 40-minute mark, the trail surface becomes much rougher and more demanding.

The trail continues making switchbacks as you work your way up the side of the ridgeline. While the trail surface has become more challenging, the pitch remains moderate. Like many smaller peaks in New England, Mount Williams has a densely forested summit. There is, however, a small clearing off to the right of the trail as you emerge from the dense forest. There's a sign posted indicating the summit and an elevation of 2,951 feet. It's about a 50-minute hike to the top from the Wilbur's Clearing parking area.

Once you've arrived, sit a moment and enjoy the view. There's just enough room for a few people to enjoy some lunch and a break, as well as the commanding views. Just be sure to take the north-bound route down to end up in the same spot. The southbound direction appears more obvious when you move from the clearing back onto the trail.

## Nearby Attractions

The towns of Williamstown and North Adams, Massachusetts, are nearby, with plenty of lodging, dining, and cultural options. You're also right in the thick of Mount Greylock State Reservation, with plenty of additional hiking and camping options.

## Directions

From MA 2 in North Adams, Massachusetts, follow Notch Road 2.3 miles to Mount Greylock State Reservation. Continue about another 2.3 miles to trailhead parking on the left (east) side of the road.

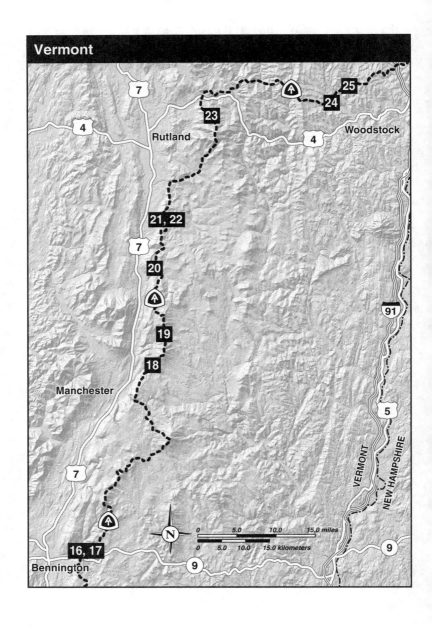

# Vermont

**THERE'S LITTLE DOUBT WHY THIS IS CALLED LITTLE ROCK POND.** (S*ee page 128.*)

SCENERY: ★ ★ ★ ★
TRAIL CONDITION: ★ ★ ★
CHILDREN: ★ ★
DIFFICULTY: ★ ★ ★ ★
SOLITUDE: ★ ★ ★ ★

THE BEGINNING OF THE HARMON HILL TRAIL WILL TEST YOUR STAMINA.

**GPS TRAILHEAD COORDINATES:** N42° 53.108' W73° 6.932'

**DISTANCE & CONFIGURATION:** 3.6-mile out-and-back

**HIKING TIME:** 2.75 hours

**HIGHLIGHTS:** Spectacular wooded grove at summit

**ELEVATION:** 2,325' at summit, 1,355' at trailhead

**ACCESS:** Parking area right off VT 9

**MAPS:** Appalachian Trail Conservancy *NH–VT Map 8* and DeLorme *VT Atlas & Gazetteer Map 21*

**CONTACT:** Green Mountain National Forest: **www.fs.usda.gov/fingerlakes**

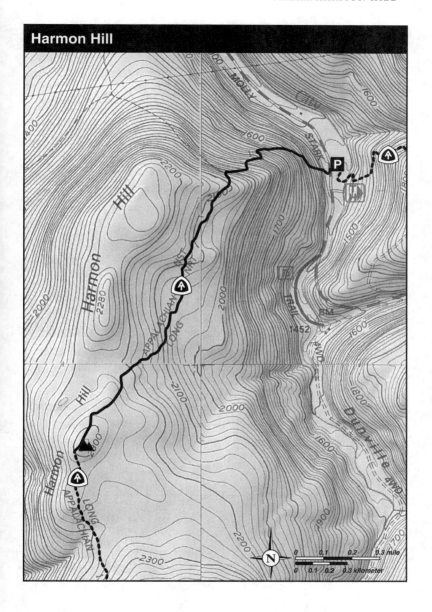

## Overview

Harmon Hill starts off with a grueling, seemingly relentless climb up a long circuitous stone stairway but ends with a placid, lush, green field and forest.

## Route Details

Vermont is known as the Green Mountain State. With that in mind, don't be lulled into a false sense of complacency when approaching a hike labeled as a hill. The first 45 minutes of the Harmon Hill hike with have you gasping for breath, your heart pounding and your legs burning.

First things first—the parking area for Harmon Hill is just off VT 9. Be extremely careful crossing the road. This is a busy state highway and cars are often flying around the bend.

The trail starts off quite steep and rocky right off the road. Long, winding stone steps guide you up the first section. The trail climbs dramatically and steeply at first and doesn't let up. The trail veers away from the road and continues its relentless ascent up steep, moss-covered stone staircases. Be extra careful here because it can be slippery even on dry days.

The series of steep stone staircases continues. You are clearly earning elevation quite rapidly in this first section of the hike. The long, stone, moss-covered stairs of uneven granite look like the stairs

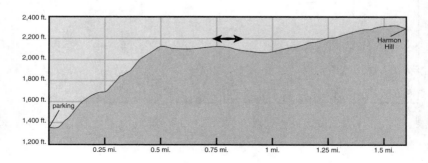

into Mordor in *The Lord of the Rings* movies. Take your time and be careful. Hikers going up and coming down often have difficulty. Not all the rocks are solidly placed either. Test them before committing your full weight.

The long, steep stone stairs continue their relentless climb up the side of Harmon Hill. The trail gives you a quick break with a brief flat section, then it's right back to the stairs. After one particularly long, steep stone staircase about 30 minutes into the hike, the trail switches back to the left. You're out of the stone stairs, but it's still steep. Then the trail switches right. After about 50 minutes of tough climbing, you begin to crest the lower hillside and the trail pitch relaxes. Enjoy the break. You've earned it.

Now the trail meanders across the hillside plateau—a relaxing ramble through a lush undergrowth of ferns and a fairly open forest overhead. This is a welcome break from the initial grueling climb. This plateau can get a bit muddy in spots. You'll come to a series of Appalachian Trail (A.T.) wooden footbridges at about 1 hour into the hike. On a hike like this, it's nice to just stop and enjoy Emerson's "wise silence of the forest."

The trail continues a nice ramble through the forest over this plateau. You're enjoying the altitude you earned earlier in the hike by lunging up that incessant set of stone stairs. The forest is fairly open and breezy in the middle part of this plateau, with some muddy sections that you'll traverse on a series of wooden A.T. footbridges.

Nearer to the top, the land dries out and the forest takes on a deep, lush character. The undergrowth of a lush bed of ferns just moments from the top and the surrounding open fields truly look like Winnie-the-Pooh's Hundred Acre Wood. On a bright summer day, the forest is a brilliant shimmering green. You'll know you've reached the top when you see an A.T. signpost and logbooks at a small clearing and trail intersection. Look around here. The forest is always scenic, but the character of the forest atop Harmon Hill is spectacular.

## Nearby Attractions

The town of Bennington, Vermont, has many lodging and dining options, and there are myriad hiking and camping options in this southern portion of the Green Mountain National Forest.

## Directions

From I-91, take Exit 2. Follow VT 9 West 34 miles. The parking area is on the right (north) shortly after you pass Woodford, Vermont. If you enter Bennington, Vermont, you've gone too far.

**MAPLE HILL IS A LONG, PEACEFUL HIKE.**

SCENERY: ★ ★ ★ ★
TRAIL CONDITION: ★ ★ ★ ★
CHILDREN: ★ ★ ★
DIFFICULTY: ★ ★ ★
SOLITUDE: ★ ★ ★ ★

**GPS TRAILHEAD COORDINATES:** N42° 53.108' W73° 6.932'

**DISTANCE & CONFIGURATION:** 4.4-mile out-and-back

**HIKING TIME:** 2.5 hours

**HIGHLIGHTS:** Trail passes through massive cracked boulder

**ELEVATION:** 2,620' at summit, 1,340' at trailhead

**ACCESS:** Parking area right off VT 9

**MAPS:** Appalachian Trail Conservancy *NH–VT Map 8* and DeLorme *VT Atlas & Gazetteer Map 21*

**CONTACT:** Green Mountain National Forest: **www.fs.usda.gov/fingerlakes**

## Maple Hill

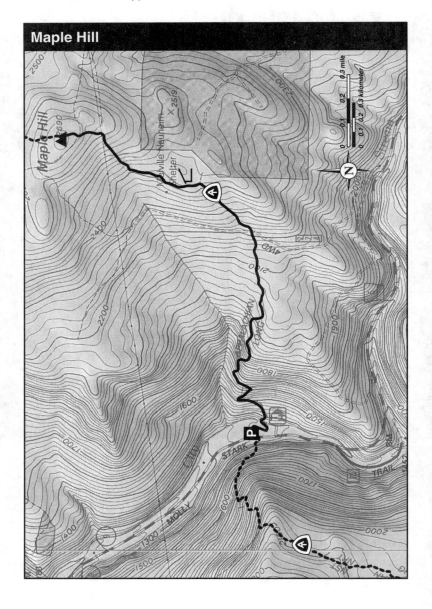

## Overview

There's not really a defined summit to Maple Hill, but the hike itself is a nice ramble through the forest.

## Route Details

The Maple Hill Trail starts at the end of the parking lot farthest from VT 9. You hike down along the river and cross over a fairly major bridge. After crossing the bridge, the trail veers to the left and follows down along the riverbank. The trail is quite flat at first. After a brief ramble along the river, the trail veers sharply to the right away from the river and up a set of stone stairs.

Here the trail begins a steady, moderate climb. The surrounding forest is very open with a high canopy providing shade. The trail isn't too well-defined here, so keep an eye out for the white blazes. The trail surface is extremely rocky, so much so that it resembles an old streambed. Ten minutes into the hike, you'll come to a moss-covered rock garden.

After that, the trail pitch increases. The trail becomes a bit steeper and is much better defined here. There's kind of a jungle-like appearance to the forest and the trail, with moss-covered rocks, dense ferns, and a high forest canopy. Even though the trail is better defined, pay attention, as it would be fairly easy to wander off-trail.

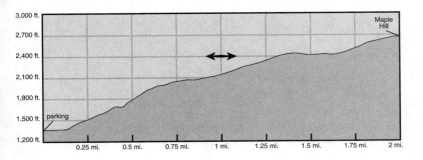

The trail continues its steady, moderate grade. Higher up on the ridge, it switches back and continues a moderate climb over a rocky surface. The trail here takes you on a steady but moderate climb with a couple of shorter steep sections. The trail switches back again. You can definitely feel as if you've gained some altitude here.

After another switchback, the trail continues wandering to the north, following along the hillside. All you can hear now is the sound of a river flowing by below. The trail surface is still quite rocky here, so do be careful as you're hiking. Continuing north, the trail passes through another rock garden of moss-covered rocks. The trail pitch also gets a bit steeper briefly.

After a couple of tighter switchbacks, the trail continues its rocky ascent. You're about 30 minutes into the hike at this point. You're getting high enough to be able to see through some of the tree-tops to the south. Then the trail passes through another rock garden, with a large rock ledge on the left. The trail is still well-defined here, if not all that well marked. You'll come to a set of stone steps, then after these the trail pitch increases and you'll go through more frequent and tighter switchbacks.

After about 40 minutes of hiking, you'll pass though this trail's most unique feature—a massive split granite boulder. And yes, the trail passes right through the middle of this huge rock. This is a great spot for a couple of pictures, as it does look quite dramatic. After passing through this massive boulder, the trail veers to the left to another couple of steep, twisting stone stairways.

Then you come to somewhat of a plateau. The trail surface is firm and smooth, and you're hiking through an open forest. The trail meanders peacefully through the woods. Then after almost 1 hour of hiking, the trail crosses over an old fire road bed. Proceed straight across to stay on the Appalachian Trail.

Shortly after crossing the old fire road, you'll come to the spur trail to the Nauheim shelter. The trail still has a gentle grade here and a smoother trail surface. Continuing, you will pass under a major set of power lines. About 10 minutes after reentering the woods on the other side of the power lines, you'll enter the Glastenbury Wilderness. Then shortly after that, you'll come to the top of Maple Hill. There's not much of a defined summit here. It's one of those situations where you'll know you've passed it when you start descending on the other side. You could turn around here, or if you wanted to extend the hike, you could continue on to Porcupine Overlook.

## Nearby Attractions

The town of Bennington, Vermont, has many lodging and dining options, and there are myriad hiking and camping options in this southern portion of the Green Mountain National Forest.

## Directions

From I-91, take Exit 2. Follow VT 9 West 34 miles. The parking area is on the right (north) shortly after you pass Woodford, Vermont. If you enter Bennington, Vermont, you've gone too far.

**BROMLEY MOUNTAIN TRAIL IS WELL USED AND EQUALLY WELL MAINTAINED.**

**GPS TRAILHEAD COORDINATES:** N43° 12.413' W72° 58.243'

**DISTANCE & CONFIGURATION:** 6-mile out-and-back

**HIKING TIME:** 3.33 hours

**HIGHLIGHTS:** Views from overlook below summit and from summit itself

**ELEVATION:** 3,260' at summit, 1,880' at trailhead

**ACCESS:** Parking area right off VT 9

**MAPS:** Appalachian Trail Conservancy *NH–VT Map 7* and DeLorme *VT Atlas & Gazetteer Map 25*

**CONTACT:** Green Mountain National Forest: **www.fs.usda.gov/fingerlakes**

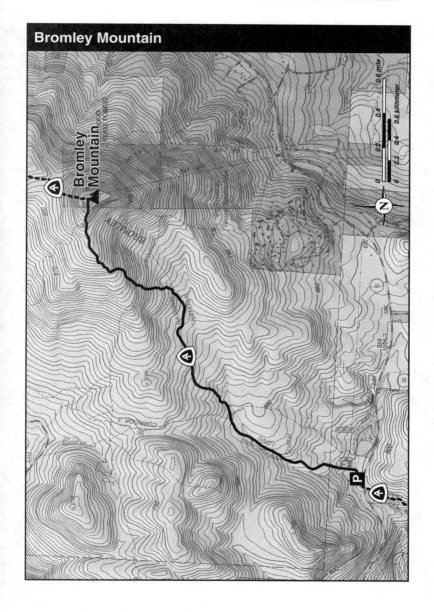

## Overview

Bromley is a good, solid hike but neither too long nor too steep to preclude bringing the whole family. There are fantastic views from the top and an overlook just below the top.

## Route Details

The Spruce Peak Trail up Bromley Mountain is the route the Appalachian Trail (A.T.) follows. There's a good-size parking area right off the north side of VT 30, so parking shouldn't be an issue. This is also the parking spot for the Vermont Association of Snow Travelers (VAST) snowmobile trail network, so it's likely to be busy year-round.

Follow the signs for the 7N snowmobile trail that leads past the signboard, and this will lead to the Spruce Peak trailhead. The trail starts out wide and flat, like a fire road. When you get to an intersection about 50 yards in, the VAST trail heads straight and the Spruce Peak Trail heads to the left. From here, it's 3 miles to the summit of Bromley.

As you head off on the true hiking trail now, it's a bit muddy in some sections. You'll pass over a series of the classic A.T. footbridges. The trail ascends steadily here but at a fairly moderate grade. Here you're hiking through a fairly dense forest. The trail itself is nice and wide and well-defined. This is a popular hiking route, so it is heavily used in the warmer months. This section of the trail follows the path

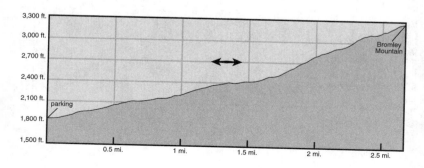

of a stream as well. About 30 minutes into the hike, you'll pass over and through a large rock garden.

The trail pitch is still fairly moderate. When you come to a larger bridge built over a major stream crossing, the trail gets a bit steeper on the far side. Just after crossing the bridge, you'll go up your first set of stone stairs. Shortly thereafter, you'll cross over a series of the long A.T. footbridges as the trail passes through a swampy zone. When you start seeing a clearing emerging on the right, be sure to stop and look, as it is a spectacularly scenic clearing amidst this swampy section. It's wet here all the time, and bugs love that, so don't forget bug stuff or you'll be carried away.

After passing by that clearing, there's another mellow stream crossing—no bridge required here. The trail maintains its moderate grade, which could explain its popularity as a day hike. It's a nice ramble through the forest over streams and along footbridges. About 45 minutes in, you'll cross over a mountain bike path. Be sure to look up because you wouldn't want to wander in front of someone flying down the road on a mountain bike.

The trail is still following the path of the stream, so there's that gentle sound in the background as you're hiking. Shortly after crossing the mountain bike path, the trail begins to steepen. You knew it was coming. Now you're steadily climbing but still at a relatively moderate pace. At about 1 hour into the hike, you're still steadily climbing and the trail passes over another set of A.T. footbridges.

After this, and a bit more than 1 hour into the hike, the trail takes a serpentine twist over a heavily root-bound section, and begins to get a bit steeper. The trail is still very well-defined here, so staying on the trail is not a problem. At 70 minutes into the hike, after a couple of tight switchbacks, you'll come to the shelter. You've come 2 miles at this point, so you have 1 mile left to the summit. Here the trail is steadily climbing over a much rockier surface.

In the final mile, there are many more switchbacks as the trail snakes its way up toward the summit of Bromley Mountain. As you navigate these switchbacks, look out through the forest and you can see you've gained significant elevation. As you get higher on the mountain, the forest starts to open up a bit. The trail surface here is still quite rough, with lots of roots and rocks.

You will come to a short spur trail off to the right to a scenic vista. This is well worth a side trip, both on the way up and the way down. The views from this open ledge are expansive. This is also an excellent place for lunch on a warm sunny day. Continuing to the summit, you'll go through a couple more switchbacks and come to a long stone-and-log staircase. You're close now. Shortly after that, you'll come out onto one of the ski trails. From there, it's just 0.3 mile to the summit and the top of the chairlift.

As you're hiking up, you'll swear that ski trail you're hiking up must be a black diamond, or at least a blue square. No, it's just a green circle.

## Nearby Attractions

The town of Manchester, Vermont, has many lodging and dining options, and there are myriad hiking and camping options in this southern portion of the Green Mountain National Forest. Emerald Lake State Forest is also nearby.

## Directions

From Manchester, Vermont, follow VT 11 East/VT 30 South for 5.8 miles. The parking area will be on the left (north) side of VT 11. If you come to the VT 11/VT 30 split, you've gone too far.

**19** # Styles Peak

SCENERY: ★ ★ ★ ★ ★
TRAIL CONDITION: ★ ★ ★
CHILDREN: ★ ★ ★
DIFFICULTY: ★ ★ ★
SOLITUDE: ★ ★ ★ ★

**THE REMOTE STYLES PEAK HIKE FINISHES WITH DRAMATIC VIEWS FROM THE SUMMIT LEDGE.**

**GPS TRAILHEAD COORDINATES:** N43° 15.465' W72° 56.304'

**DISTANCE & CONFIGURATION:** 2.8-mile out-and-back

**HIKING TIME:** 2 hours

**HIGHLIGHTS:** Epic views from summit

**ELEVATION:** 3,394' at summit, 2,452' at trailhead

**ACCESS:** Parking area off Mad Tom Notch Road

**MAPS:** Appalachian Trail Conservancy *NH–VT Map 7* and DeLorme *VT Atlas & Gazetteer Map 25*

**CONTACT:** Green Mountain National Forest: **www.fs.usda.gov/fingerlakes**

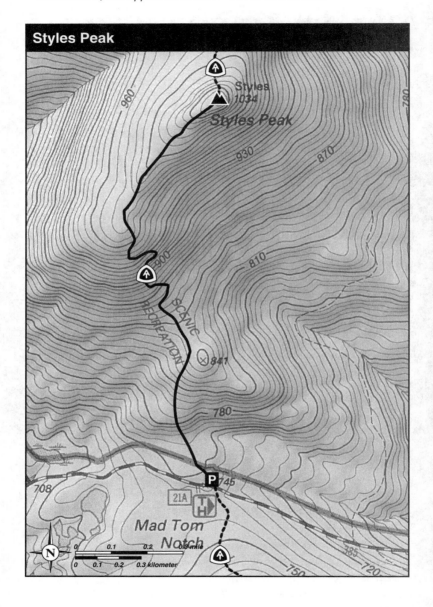

Styles Peak

## Overview

The hike up Styles Peak has many dramatic switchbacks and rock formations, and the granite ledge overlook at the top affords sweeping views of the Green Mountain National Forest.

## Route Details

Just finding the trailhead for Styles Peak is a trip into the backcountry. You'll follow Mad Tom Notch Road, which is a long, winding dirt forest road. From the parking area off the side of the road a few miles in, the trail is 1.4 miles to the top of Styles Peak.

The trail leads off from a clearing across from the parking lot with a pump, a small map, and a signpost. The trail starts off at a gentle grade with a firm, hard-packed surface. The trail is quite well-defined and somewhat well marked. Here the trail snakes through a dense, low forest of mostly birch and pine.

After just a few minutes of hiking, the trail pitch increases to a moderate grade. The trail surface is still hard packed and rocky. The trail grade quickly becomes much steeper as you continue. After the first steep pitch, you'll come to a set of stone stairs and a large boulder on the right. After another set of stone stairs—this one a twisting S turn—the trail mellows slightly.

The forest here is still quite dense, both overhead and the ground cover. About 20 minutes in, you'll come to another spaced-out

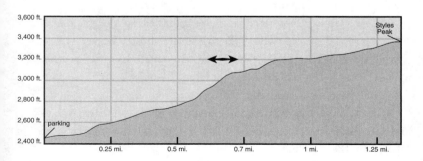

125

**SECTIONS OF THE STYLES PEAK TRAIL ARE QUITE STEEP AND ROCKY.**

set of stone steps that follows the curve of the trail. The trail continues its steady yet moderate ascent.

Farther along, the trail rises and falls but continues climbing overall. The steeper and mellower sections give you a bit of a break as you're hiking. The trail here is both well-defined and well marked. At the 25-minute mark, you'll come to another set of stone steps that takes you up a brief, steeper pitch. The trail is still quite narrow and winding and passing through dense undergrowth.

At slightly more than 30 minutes into the hike, the trail makes a dramatic 90-degree switchback to the left and continues its sustained, steady climb. Shortly thereafter, you'll come to another switchback as the trail snakes its way up the hillside. At this point, the trail becomes significantly steeper and remains that way. Looking out through the slightly more open forest, you can realize you've already earned some altitude. The trail continues following along the course of the ridgeline.

Now that you're higher up on the ridge, the switchbacks are tighter than before. The trail itself is still quite narrow, with a rough surface punctuated by roots and rocks. After about 55 minutes of hiking, you come to the top plateau of the ridgeline. The trail pitch mellows out quite a bit here, and you pass over a series of Appalachian Trail (A.T.) footbridges. There's a lovely low-canopy pine forest up here.

You'll traverse another A.T. footbridge after the trail takes a short, steep drop down into a slightly muddy area. It can feel a bit confusing as to whether you are at the top or not, but continue. The summit plateau is relatively flat. The trail will take you up and down and through this massive granite rock pile. You're almost there. Shortly after you climb through this puzzle of giant granite boulders, you'll come to an overview clearing with dramatic views. The view from here of the Vermont backcountry is worth every step.

## Nearby Attractions

The town of Manchester, Vermont, has many lodging and dining options, and there are myriad hiking and camping options in this southern portion of the Green Mountain National Forest. Emerald Lake State Forest is also nearby.

## Directions

From Manchester, Vermont, follow VT 11 East for 9.8 miles. Make a slight left onto Main Street, and in 0.3 mile, turn left onto Hapgood Pond Road. In 1 mile, bear left onto North Road, and in 0.8 mile turn left onto Mad Tom Notch Road (a dirt road). Follow this 2.1 miles to the parking area on the left (across from a clearing with a water pump and map kiosk).

SCENERY: ★ ★ ★ ★
TRAIL CONDITION: ★ ★ ★
CHILDREN: ★ ★ ★
DIFFICULTY: ★ ★ ★
SOLITUDE: ★ ★ ★

**THIS HIKE FOLLOWS A STREAM TO LITTLE ROCK POND.**

**GPS TRAILHEAD COORDINATES:** N43° 22.360' W72° 57.754'

**DISTANCE & CONFIGURATION:** 4.2-mile out-and-back

**HIKING TIME:** 2.33 hours

**HIGHLIGHTS:** Little Rock Pond

**ELEVATION:** 1,850' at pond, 1,800' at trailhead

**ACCESS:** Large parking area off Forest Road 10 (Brooklyn Road), which may be closed during the winter months

**MAPS:** Appalachian Trail Conservancy *NH–VT Map 7* and DeLorme *VT Atlas & Gazetteer Map 25*

**CONTACT:** Green Mountain National Forest: **www.fs.usda.gov/fingerlakes**

## Little Rock Pond

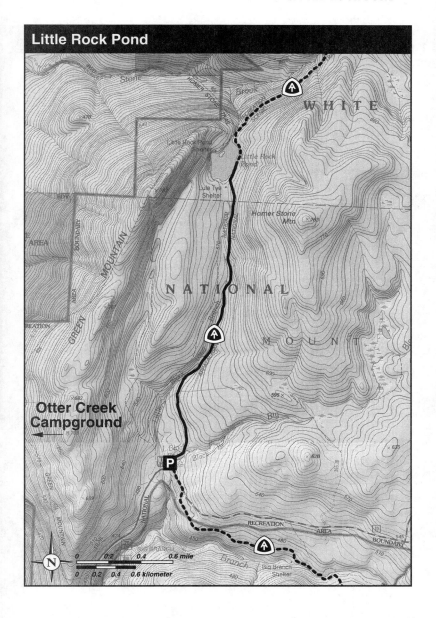

Otter Creek
Campground

## Overview

This is an excellent hike for younger kids, as there's no appreciable elevation gain and the hike ends at the stunning shores of Little Rock Pond.

## Route Details

The ramble out to Little Rock Pond is relaxing and quite scenic. This is truly a great hike for the younger hikers in your group. And being at the pond at the apex of the hike is well worth every step.

To get there, you'll follow FR 10 out of Danby, Vermont. This road twists and winds and climbs up to the Appalachian Trail–Long Trail parking lot on the right (east). This is a good-size parking area with space for 25 cars. The trailhead is right across the road from the parking area. There's also an outhouse there if you need one.

Follow the sounds of a rushing brook to the trailhead. The trail starts off quite rocky and root-bound with a mild pitch. This is quite a popular trail, as it is fairly gentle. This is an excellent hike for smaller children—it has rocky sections but never too much climbing.

About five minutes into the hike, you'll ascend a set of log steps and continue climbing at a truly gentle, relaxed pace. The entire first section of this trail parallels the stream. The trail surface is still quite rocky and uneven but well-defined and easy to follow. About 10 minutes into the hike, you'll pass a campsite for thru-hikers on the left side of the trail.

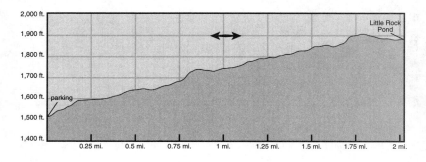

The trail continues its easy ramble through the fairly dense forest with dense undergrowth on either side of the trail. The forest is a mix of birch, maple, and conifers. The trail itself is very well-defined, as this is a popular trail that sees a lot of hikers. The trail here also gets less rocky and more firmly hard packed. This entire trail must be a welcome relief for weary thru-hikers. And it's certainly an exciting hike for smaller kids.

At about 20 minutes into the hike, the trail has moved away from the brook it was following at the beginning to following the course of another brook on the left side of the trail. The sound of the brook splashing by makes a nice, peaceful sound track to your walk in the woods. Shortly after the trail starts following this brook, you'll cross a metal I-beam bridge over the brook to the other side.

Now the trail follows this brook quite closely. The brook-side route of the trail means it can get a bit rockier with more exposed roots, but it still follows a predominantly flat grade. It can be slick in the wet spots, so watch your step. After you hike a few minutes down the far side of the brook, the trail crosses back over—this time over several large, flat rocks. The trail is a bit less well-defined and marked here, so keep an eye out for the white blazes.

After this crossing, the trail is certainly less well-defined. Just pay attention to where it's heading and check for blazes. It's still basically following the stream, though, so you can't wander too far off. Overall, this trail is a fairly straight out-and-back to Little Rock Pond. Farther down, the trail veers away from the brook and the trail surface gets a bit firmer but remains fairly rocky.

At the 40-minute mark, you'll cross over a series of Appalachian Trail (A.T.) footbridges that will traverse a short swampy section. The wet areas and the streams mean this trail can get buggy, so be sure to have your favorite bug stuff for you and the kids. Shortly after this series of A.T. footbridges, the trail rejoins the brook and once again gets much rockier. After 55 minutes of hiking, you'll come to a spectacularly scenic swampy clearing. This clearing looks like something out of *Jurassic Park,* with short, moss-covered trees hanging in the swamp and lots of low vegetation.

After passing this clearing, you'll go over another series of A.T. footbridges. The whole ground is quite damp in here. Those footbridges go a long way toward minimizing erosion, especially on such a popular trail. After 1 hour and 10 minutes, you'll come to the shore of Little Rock Pond. You can quickly see a small boulder just offshore that is likely the pond's namesake. Little Rock Pond is quite beautiful. If your gang has the time and energy, there's also the Little Rock Pond Loop that encircles the pond. Otherwise, you can turn back here after enjoying the placid waters of Little Rock Pond.

## Nearby Attractions

You're roughly equidistant from Manchester or Rutland, Vermont, here. There are many lodging and dining options in each town. You're also close to Emerald Lake State Park and the Otter Creek Campground.

## Directions

From US 7 in Mount Tabor, Vermont, follow FR 10 (also called Brooklyn Road) 3.1 miles to the parking area on the right (south) side of the road. This road may be closed during the winter.

SCENERY: ★ ★ ★ ★ ★
TRAIL CONDITION: ★ ★ ★
CHILDREN: ★ ★ ★
DIFFICULTY: ★ ★ ★ ★
SOLITUDE: ★ ★ ★ ★

**THE OCCASIONALLY DEMANDING HIKE UP WHITE ROCK LEDGE WILL REWARD YOU WITH AN INTERESTING FIND.**

**GPS TRAILHEAD COORDINATES:** N43° 27.632' W72° 55.172'

**DISTANCE & CONFIGURATION:** 5.6-mile out-and-back

**HIKING TIME:** 2.75 hours

**HIGHLIGHTS:** Surreal cairn garden at summit, views from White Rock Ledge

**ELEVATION:** 2,680' at summit, 1,130' at trailhead

**ACCESS:** Parking off VT 140

**MAPS:** Appalachian Trail Conservancy *NH–VT Map 7* and DeLorme *VT Atlas & Gazetteer Map 29*

**CONTACT:** Green Mountain National Forest: **www.fs.usda.gov/fingerlakes**

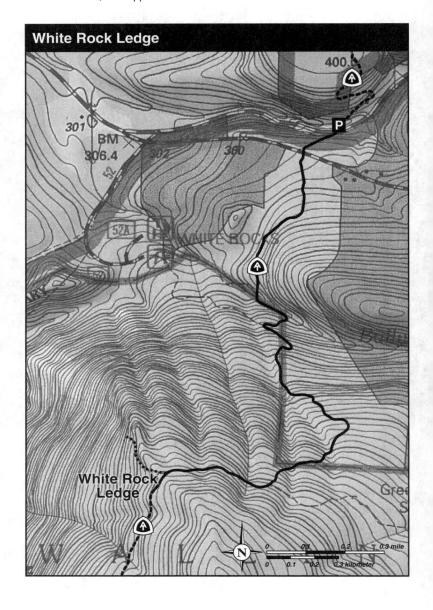

## Overview

A moderately strenuous hike takes you to the rounded summit of White Rock Ledge, where you can marvel at the cairn garden and the views from the White Rock Ledge overlook.

## Route Details

The hike up to White Rock Ledge starts out heading over a burly wooden bridge over Roaring Brook that follows the course of VT 140 down the mountainside. This is a good place to refill water if you need to, but of course only if you treat the water or use a filter.

After crossing the bridge, the trail veers to the right to a steep initial climb up a short, rocky pitch. This is kind of a tough warm-up for the rest of the hike. After the first set of stone stairs, you'll pass through a fascinating rock garden and then another set of stone stairs. After that intense introduction, the trail crosses over a well-used dirt road.

After that road crossing, the Appalachian Trail (A.T.) reenters the woods, which has a junglelike feeling with lots of moss and ferns. The trail has an uneven, rocky surface here, so step carefully. There's also a much more moderate pitch here, as compared to the initial lunge. The trail rolls up through the lush, dense forest, through a couple of small ravines, and past massive boulder fields. It's truly quite a scenic hike in this section.

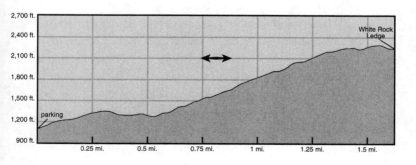

**A SURREAL AND SPOOKY CAIRN GARDEN AWAITS YOU AT THE TOP OF WHITE ROCK LEDGE.**

If you look down into the ravines to the right as you're hiking up, you realize you've already earned a fair bit of elevation. Farther along the ridgeline, the trail opens up a bit. There are still a lot of roots and rocks on the trail as it maintains a steady, moderate climb. There's less undergrowth here and a high forest canopy. Keep an eye out for the white blazes, as it would be fairly easy to wander off-trail. The trail is fairly well-defined, but the forest floor is quite open.

The trail turns left and passes by a brook rushing down through the rocks. The trail also pitches up considerably and consistently. The falls down to the right are spectacular—both in sight and in sound. The trail does eventually cross the brook and then veers to the right, heading downstream. The trail is quite rocky and steep here, so watch your footing. You'll also head up another set of stone stairs. You're about 25 minutes into the hike at this point.

Then the trail banks up to the left, heading up more stone stairs. As this is part of a runoff, the stone stairs are often wet and a bit muddy, so be careful here. After this turn, you'll come to an intersection with the Keewaydin Trail. Follow the A.T. and Long Trail to the left to head for White Rock Ledge. The trail here is a sustained moderate-to-steep pitch. It's also quite rocky and can be wet at times. The trail is also better marked and defined in this section.

After this long, straight, steep section, the trail makes a wide switchback to the right and maintains its steep-to-moderate pitch.

The pitch levels out briefly, then bends to the left and picks up again. In this whole section, the trail varies from steep to moderate, but always over a rocky surface. The trail continues as such, following a couple of switchbacks and shorter turns as well.

After you pass a turnoff for the short spur trail to the Greenwall shelter, the trail narrows and continues to run over an uneven, rocky surface. The trail winds through the dense forest on either side. There's a dense, sylvan, almost boreal quality to the forest here. This section is the final lunge to the summit plateau of White Rock Ledge.

When you emerge from the narrow corridor of dense conifers, you will come to something you won't see anywhere else. There is a spectacular and surreal garden containing dozens of cairns of all shapes and sizes crafted from the milky quartz that makes up White Rock Ledge. Take a moment to wander through the cairns. People must have been building these for years. There's even a cairn built up in the Y-shaped split of a large tree. It's about 1 hour and 40 minutes to this summit plateau with its epic cairn garden.

There's a short spur trail leading down to the White Rock Ledge overlook, which is also worth the extra trip. It's a 0.2-mile side trip down the blue-blazed White Rock Cliff Trail, so it will take another 10 minutes or so. Both the views from the White Rock Ledge overlook and from the amazing cairn garden make this a hike you won't want to miss.

## Nearby Attractions

You're closest to Rutland, Vermont, here and numerous lodging and dining options.

## Directions

From US 7 in Wallingford, Vermont, follow VT 140 for almost 4 miles to the small roadside parking area on the right at the trailhead or about 50 feet farther to a larger parking area to the left off VT 140.

# Bear Mountain

**BEAR MOUNTAIN TRAIL PASSES BY SOME IMPRESSIVE ROCK FORMATIONS.**

SCENERY: ★ ★ ★
TRAIL CONDITION: ★ ★ ★ ★
CHILDREN: ★ ★ ★
DIFFICULTY: ★ ★ ★
SOLITUDE: ★ ★ ★

**GPS TRAILHEAD COORDINATES:** N43° 27.632' W72° 55.172'

**DISTANCE & CONFIGURATION:** 4.2-mile out-and-back

**HIKING TIME:** 1.75 hours

**HIGHLIGHTS:** Dense scenic forest, with some overviews

**ELEVATION:** 2,240' at summit, 1,130' at trailhead

**ACCESS:** Parking off VT 140

**MAPS:** Appalachian Trail Conservancy *NH–VT Map 6* and DeLorme *VT Atlas & Gazetteer Map 29*

**CONTACT:** Green Mountain National Forest: **www.fs.usda.gov/fingerlakes**

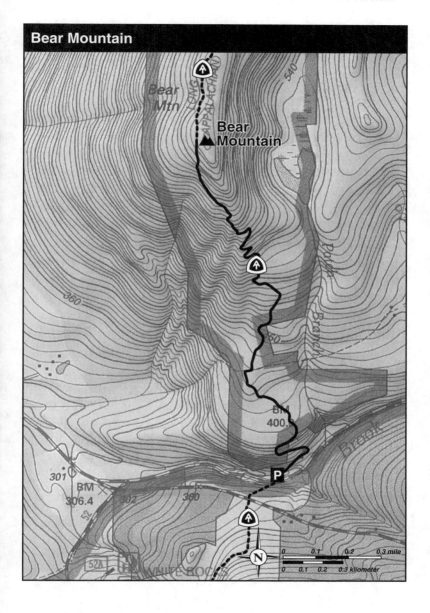

Bear Mountain

## Overview

The Bear Mountain hike is a nice, gentle ramble through the forest.

## Route Details

Bear Mountain is just across VT 140 from the White Rock Ledge hike. If you start early in the day, you could have time to do them both in one day. There's a small parking area off to the right side of VT 140, room for four or five cars. You'll park here for either the Bear Mountain or the White Rock Ledge hikes. There's another parking spot on the left a bit farther up with room for at least 15 cars. Break-ins are possible, so don't leave any valuables in plain view.

The trail leads into the dense pine forest at a moderate grade. The dense forest means it can also be buggy, so be prepared. The trail surface is firm and hard packed. The trail here is also well marked and well-defined. There's a nice little campsite just off the trail to the right shortly after you begin the hike.

After 10 minutes or so, you'll come to the larger parking area up off of VT 140 on the left. The Bear Mountain Trail leads out of the north side of the larger parking area. The trail starts right off with a moderate, sustained pitch. The trail here is straight and wide and well-defined. After about 15 minutes of hiking, the trail makes a sweeping right-hand turn and begins snaking through the forest.

A bit farther along, the trail follows the course of an old stone wall. After the trail heads away from the stone wall, it becomes

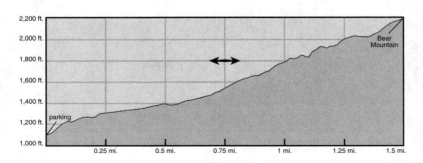

narrower, windier, and more root-bound. After 25 minutes into the hike, the trail gets rockier and passes over an old streambed. The pitch increases slightly and the trail narrows and passes through a dense ground cover.

Then the trail begins a series of gentle switchbacks as it follows a sustained, moderate pitch up the hillside. The trail is also still quite well-defined and well marked in this section. The surrounding forest is a young, fairly dense forest of mostly slender birch, maples, and conifers with heavy undergrowth as well.

At the 40-minute mark, the trail splits with the blue-blazed Domed Ledge Vista Trail. The Appalachian Trail continues to the right. After that, you'll pass through a couple of sweeping switchbacks as you continue the sustained, relatively moderate ascent.

As you get higher up, the switchbacks get a bit tighter and more frequent. At about 55 minutes into the hike, you'll pass over another stone staircase. From here, there's a dramatic, open view of the forest below. The switchbacks continue to get tighter as you continue the hike. About 5 minutes after that stone staircase, you'll pass a huge boulder on the right of the trail. This is also a great spot for a view of the forest below and what you've climbed already.

After passing that large boulder, the trail takes a straight shot along a ridgeline. You are just below the top of Bear Mountain here. After this long, straight section, the trail veers right for a brief final lunge to the top. The top of Bear Mountain is blanketed with dense ferns and a fairly dense surrounding forest. It doesn't have a truly well-defined summit, but you'll know you've passed it if you start descending on the other side.

## Nearby Attractions

You're closest to Rutland, Vermont, here and numerous lodging and dining options.

**BEAR MOUNTAIN TRAIL IS GENTLE FOR MOST OF THE HIKE.**

## Directions

From US 7 in Wallingford, Vermont, follow VT 140 for almost 4 miles to the small roadside parking area on the right at the trailhead or about 50 feet farther to a larger parking area to the left off VT 140.

> SCENERY: ★ ★ ★ ★
> TRAIL CONDITION: ★ ★ ★
> CHILDREN: ★ ★ ★
> DIFFICULTY: ★ ★ ★
> SOLITUDE: ★ ★ ★ ★

**THE CABIN AT PICO CAMP IS A PERFECT REST SPOT.**

**GPS TRAILHEAD COORDINATES:** N43° 39.972' W72° 50.937'

**DISTANCE & CONFIGURATION:** 5.8-mile out-and-back

**HIKING TIME:** 4.75 hours

**HIGHLIGHTS:** Views from Pico Camp and summit

**ELEVATION:** 3,957' at summit, 2,150' at trailhead

**ACCESS:** Parking right off US 4

**MAPS:** Appalachian Trail Conservancy *NH–VT Map 6* and DeLorme *VT Atlas & Gazetteer Map 30*

**CONTACT:** Green Mountain National Forest: **www.fs.usda.gov/fingerlakes**

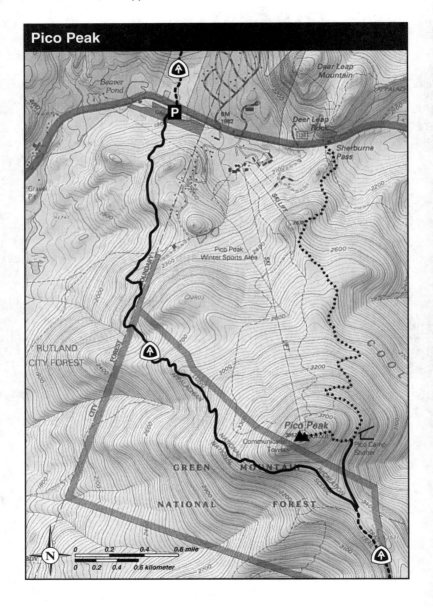

## Overview

Pico Peak is a solid hike through varied forests with fantastic views from Pico Camp and the summit.

## Route Details

It's always a thrill to be hiking up the backside of a mountain that is host to a ski area. During the Pico hike, the woods are so dense and the trail is so long—wrapping around the back of the mountain—that you won't know you're at a ski area until you emerge from the woods at the very summit.

Down at the trailhead, the trail initially leads out of the north side of the parking area. It follows along the road for a bit and then veers into the woods. Then you immediately come to a large footbridge. The hike begins in earnest after crossing that bridge into the woods.

After you cross over the footbridge, the Appalachian Trail (A.T.) bears to the left, and Catamount Trail heads to the right. The trail surface is covered with roots, but the path itself is quite well-defined and well marked. The trail soon passes over a couple of A.T. footbridges, and then it gets rockier and slightly steeper. The route now maintains a steady, moderate climb.

The trail surface is still covered with roots and rocks, which can make it a little tough to follow. Just keep an eye on the white blazes. It can also be quite slippery on a wet day, so watch your step.

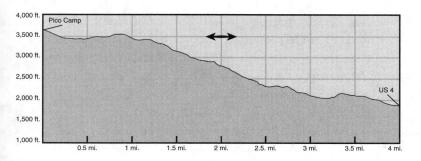

**PICO PEAK TRAIL OVERLAPS CATAMOUNT TRAIL IN SOME SPOTS.**

The forest here is a brilliant blend of hardwoods—mostly maple and birch. At about 15 minutes into the hike, the trail pitches up a bit and crosses over a short stone staircase. After this, the trail gets narrower as it winds through the forest. You're not so much making switchbacks, just winding to the left and right through the forest.

Here the forest canopy is fairly open and high, the brilliant shimmering greens of the leaves letting lots of light down to the forest floor. After about 20 minutes, you'll come to the base of a massive, moss-covered rock ledge, which makes for a dramatic sight. The trail passes by just below the ledge. Shortly before passing this huge rock ledge, the trail dips a bit before continuing its ascent. The trail is still fairly narrow, twisty, and rough with roots and rocks. It maintains a steady but moderate ascent.

The trail continues to roll up and down along the ridgeline. There are several ridges in all directions leading up to the peak of Pico. After about 35 minutes, the trail descends a stone staircase through the loosely spaced forest. You can start to see Pico Peak now through the trees. You realize you still have a fair amount of hiking to do to reach the peak. Shortly after this, cross over a small stream running through a culvert and begin a steady climb again.

The trail is fairly well marked and well-defined here, but it would still behoove you to pay attention to the white blazes to stay on the trail. At the 45-minute mark, you'll pass through a cleared-out hillside with a lot of downed trees. These are likely victims of Hurricane Irene, which tore up the Connecticut River Valley deep into northern Vermont in 2011. The trail surface and definition is variable here, so mind the blazes.

After this section, the trail continues to ascend in earnest. Now you're hiking up and along a spectacular older-growth forest along the hillside. The forest character is quite dramatic here. The trail is also steadily increasing in pitch here. The trail switches back and forth and continues its steady ascent. After about 1 hour, you'll pass through a large rock garden of moss-covered boulders. After that, the trail continues its serpentine climb up the hillside. The trail is quite rocky and less well-defined here, so keep an eye on the blazes. Shortly after passing through that rock garden, you'll come to another one. Here the trail continues its sustained climb.

After about 65 minutes of hiking, you'll pass another steep, moss-covered rock ledge. This is an impressive sight worth a picture or two. After you pass this ledge, the trail goes up a couple of steeper stone stairs and switchbacks. The trail is definitely increasing in steepness here and sustaining that pitch. After 1 hour and 15 minutes, you'll cross over another dramatically beautiful stream and continue on.

Here the trail passes through a more open forest of mostly maple and birch. At about three-fifths of the way up, you'll pass the turnoff for an A.T. shelter. The trail is narrow and well-defined here, so it's easy to follow. After 1 hour and 45 minutes or so, you'll emerge from the hardwood forest into what feels like a cathedral of conifers. This is near the summit plateau. The trail is narrow and circuitous through here.

At the 2-hour-and-20-minute mark, you'll come to an intersection with the Shelburne Pass Trail. From here, it's a 0.5-mile detour off the A.T. to get to the Pico Camp. The A.T. continues toward the Killington ridge. From the Pico Camp, which is a great place to stop for lunch or a break, it's another 0.4 mile to the peak of the Pico Mountain ski area. The trail from the intersection point to the Pico Camp is fairly moderate but gets significantly steeper in the final lunge to the summit of Pico.

## Nearby Attractions

The Killington, Vermont, area is nearby, with numerous lodging, dining, and other recreation options. You're also close to Gifford Woods State Park, which has a lovely hike through an old-growth forest just across the street.

## Directions

From I-89, take Exit 1. Follow US 4 West 10.4 miles, and then turn left to stay on US 4. Go another 22.6 miles. Go past the trailhead parking directly across from the Inn at Long Trail, and the trailhead parking area will be on the left (west) side of US 4. This parking area specifically states that it's for the A.T., the Long Trail, and the Catamount Trail (Vermont's long-distance ski trail).

| | |
| --- | --- |
| SCENERY: ★ ★ ★ ★ |
| TRAIL CONDITION: ★ ★ ★ ★ |
| CHILDREN: ★ ★ ★ |
| DIFFICULTY: ★ ★ ★ |
| SOLITUDE: ★ ★ ★ ★ |

**THE TRAILHEAD FOR DANA HILL IS VERY WELL MARKED AND CLOSE TO THE ROAD, SO YOU CAN'T MISS IT.**

**GPS TRAILHEAD COORDINATES:** N43° 39.300' W72° 33.963'

**DISTANCE & CONFIGURATION:** 1.6-mile out-and-back

**HIKING TIME:** 1.33 hours

**HIGHLIGHTS:** Massive grove of wildflowers at top

**ELEVATION:** 1,530' at summit, 880' at trailhead

**ACCESS:** Parking area off to left (west) of VT 12

**MAPS:** Appalachian Trail Conservancy *NH–VT Map 5* and DeLorme *VT Atlas & Gazetteer Map 31*

**CONTACT:** Appalachian Mountain Club: **outdoors.org**

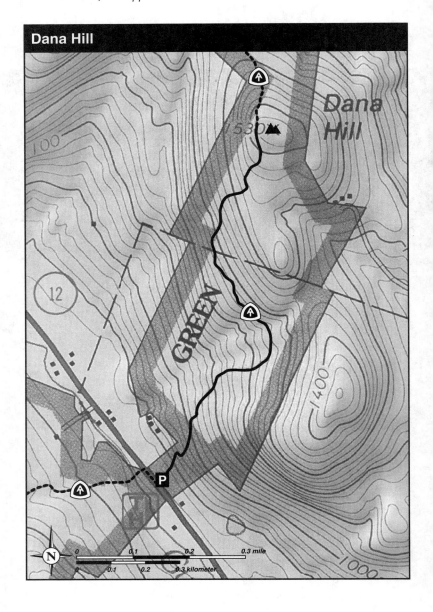

## Overview

Hiking up Dana Hill brings you through some scenic forest, a field near the top, and a grove of white wildflowers at the rounded summit cap.

## Route Details

There is a nice, safe parking area for the Dana Hill trailhead tucked down off VT 12 with room for probably eight cars. There's a pretty, solid footbridge leading north, but Dana Hill Trail takes you to the south. The trail starts off following a deep, shady grove of ferns along the river. Then you'll cross over VT 12. Do so cautiously. It's not the busiest road in the world, but when vehicles do come by, they're moving right along.

Once you enter the woods on the south side of VT 12, you'll start off with a fairly steep climb. The trail surface is firm, hard-packed dirt, which is a good thing because it is quite steep and at a side angle here. The path takes you through a grove of young maple trees. The trail takes a couple of switchbacks as it continues its fairly steep initial ascent.

You continue along this steep and steady climb until you reach what appears to be an old fire roadbed after about 10 minutes of hiking. Here the path gets much wider and the pitch mellows out slightly. The trail follows the old roadbed toward the left and uphill. The pitch may be more moderate on this old roadbed, but it's still steady climbing. The trail here is quite well-defined and well marked. It takes a couple of slow, gentle bends to the right and continues its steady ascent.

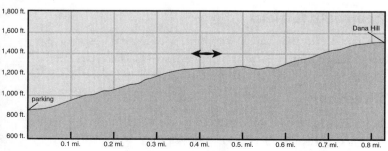

Continuing upward, the trail becomes a bit narrower and the forest opens up a bit with much less undergrowth. The forest canopy here is fairly medium height. The trail continues its steady, moderate ascent. Shortly thereafter, the pitch eases somewhat as the path bears left and takes you through a large drainage area and toward a small rise directly ahead.

The trail passes up and over this small rise and continues winding its way along the hillside. The surface here is still hard packed, but there are some roots poking through. The trail rambles up and down along the hillside, then veers slightly to the right and continues a steadier climb.

Then the trail begins another moderate, sustained ascent as it snakes to the left and right, working its way up. As you look up through the trees, you can see some more sky and what looks like a clearing. And, indeed, the trail comes out of the woods into another spectacular, open, grassy field, high up on the side of Dana Hill. There's a slightly shaky wooden foot ramp to get up and over a barbed wire fence.

The trail then passes along the left border of this field and continues climbing toward the top of the hill. Higher up, you reenter the forest after crossing back over that barbed wire fence. Once you're back into the woods, you're almost at the high point of Dana Hill. Hike another 100 yards or so to a spectacular grove of what looks like Queen Anne's lace at the rounded top of Dana Hill. This bed of white flowers is surrounded by a grove of spruce, which makes for quite a scenic hilltop.

## Nearby Attractions

You're close to Woodstock, Vermont, with several upscale lodging and dining options. You're also not far from Quechee State Park.

## Directions

From US 4 in Woodstock, Vermont, follow VT 12 North 3.9 miles to the parking area on the left (west) side of the road.

**25** # Dupuis Hill

| SCENERY: ★ ★ ★ ★ |
| TRAIL CONDITION: ★ ★ ★ |
| CHILDREN: ★ ★ ★ |
| DIFFICULTY: ★ ★ |
| SOLITUDE: ★ ★ ★ ★ |

**YOU'LL FIND THIS LUSH SCENIC GROVE ON THE DUPUIS HILL HIKE.**

**GPS TRAILHEAD COORDINATES:** N43° 40.850' W72° 31.579'

**DISTANCE & CONFIGURATION:** 3.6-mile out-and-back

**HIKING TIME:** 1.33 hours

**HIGHLIGHTS:** Scenic fields

**ELEVATION:** 1,730' at summit, 1,455' at trailhead

**ACCESS:** Parking right off Pomfret Road

**MAPS:** Appalachian Trail Conservancy *NH–VT Map 5* and DeLorme *VT Atlas & Gazetteer Map 30*

**CONTACT:** Appalachian Mountain Club: **outdoors.org**

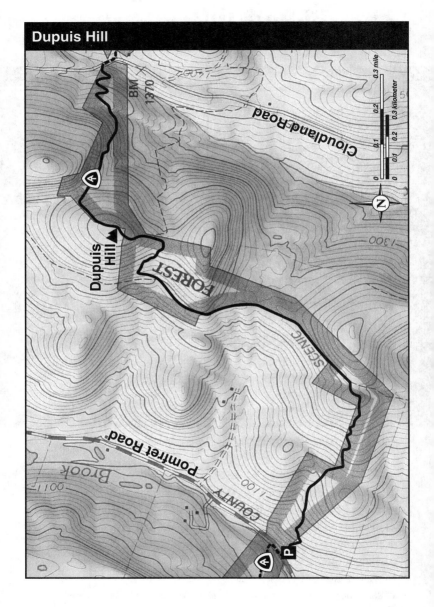

Dupuis Hill

## Overview

This is more of a ramble through the forest than an up-and-down peak hike, but it takes you through some spectacularly scenic open fields.

## Route Details

The Dupuis Hill trail starts off crossing a narrow bridge over a small brook. Then the trail hooks to the right and emerges through the trees into a beautiful open field. The well-defined trail follows along the side of the field and then reenters the woods at the other end.

Once you're back in the forest, the trail begins a steady yet moderate ascent. You're hiking through a forest canopy of tall slender pines, so lots of sunlight filters down through the trees to the forest floor. Ten minutes into the hike, you'll cross over the remnants of an old stone wall. These have been here since most of New England was farmland. At this point, you can still hear an occasional car on Pomfret Road, but the sounds of the forest are overtaking the sounds of humanity.

This is an exceptionally scenic trail and surrounding forest through which you're hiking. The trail maintains a moderate pitch and is well marked here with white blazes. The trail surface is smooth and hard and cushioned by a blanket of pine needles. This would certainly be a good hike for younger kids.

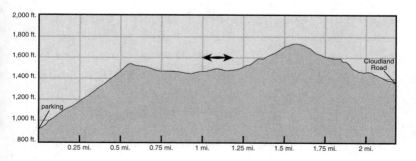

A bit farther into the forest, you'll come to another stream crossing where one of the better options for getting to the other side is walking across a large felled tree. On the other side of the stream, the trail continues up the hillside over a muddy patch. Keep an eye out for the blazes because they seem a bit loosely spaced in here. It would be easier to wander off-trail here more than anywhere else on this hike thus far.

After the stream crossing, the trail winds up and down through the woods and becomes more well-defined and well marked. The trail surface is still dry and firm with a few roots poking through. The forest overhead is a bit more loosely spaced in here. The trail meanders back and forth through the forest at a nice, relaxed pace.

After a brief ramble, the trail veers dramatically to the left and follows along the side of a ridgeline. Watch your step here as the hillside is fairly steep to the right of the trail. A fall here would certainly result in a bit of a slide. The trail follows along the top of this moderate ravine for a brief period. Farther on, the ground to either side of the trail evens out after about 50 yards or so.

The character of the trail and the surrounding forest is still spectacular—looking like a set from *The Lord of the Rings*. The trail is still well-defined if not as well marked. This doesn't seem to be a heavily used trail. The trail continues skirting around the hillside, the true top of Dupuis Hill. After about 30 minutes of hiking, you'll come to a rounded plateau. After this, the trail starts descending, so this seems to be the highest you will reach on Dupuis Hill. It's worth it to continue to Cloudland Road, which means you will head not only up and over Dupuis Hill but also through some spectacular forest scenery.

After about 40 minutes of hiking, you'll emerge from the forest again into a lush, open field. This one is clearly not maintained for agriculture but is full of wildflowers, tall grasses, and trees. The field is silent except for the buzzing and humming of all the insects and birds resident in this field. The scenery is just breathtaking as you descend through the field on a narrow but well-defined corridor. On the other side of the field, you'll cross over a few more Appalachian

Trail (A.T.) footbridges that take you over a boggy section. The trail pitch here is quite gentle. After 50 minutes, you'll come to the dirt road that is Cloudland Road. You can turn around here and head back through the forest.

## Nearby Attractions

You're close to the town of Woodstock, Vermont, which has several upscale lodging and dining options. You're also not far from Quechee State Park.

## Directions

From Woodstock, Vermont, follow VT 12 about 1.5 miles to where Pomfret Road forks off to the right toward South Pomfret, Vermont. Drive through South Pomfret almost 3.5 miles to roadside parking on the right (east) side of the road at the trailhead crossing.

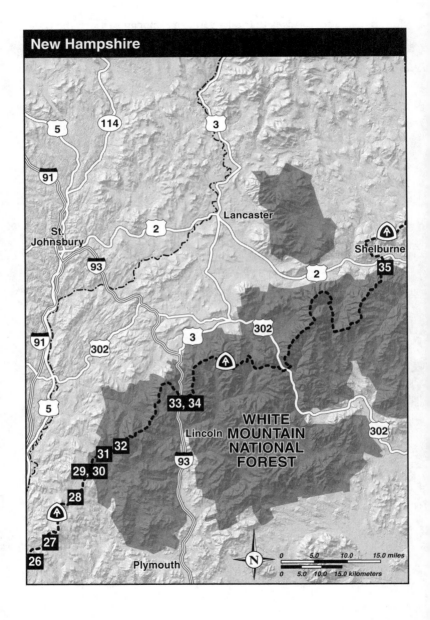

# New Hampshire

**HIKING FROM SOUTH PEAK TO THE DRAMATIC NORTH PEAK ON MOUNT MOOSILAUKE** *(See page 190.)*

# 26

# Holts Ledges

SCENERY: ★ ★ ★ ★
TRAIL CONDITION: ★ ★ ★
CHILDREN: ★ ★ ★
DIFFICULTY: ★ ★ ★
SOLITUDE: ★ ★ ★

**THE VIEW FROM ATOP HOLTS LEDGES IS BREATHTAKING.**

**GPS TRAILHEAD COORDINATES:** N43° 47.050' W72° 5.873'

**DISTANCE & CONFIGURATION:** 3.4-mile out-and-back

**HIKING TIME:** 2.75 hours

**HIGHLIGHTS:** Epic views from top

**ELEVATION:** 2,110' at summit, 920' at trailhead

**ACCESS:** Parking on left just before Dartmouth Skiway

**MAPS:** Appalachian Trail Conservancy *NH–VT Map 5* and DeLorme *NH Atlas & Gazetteer Map 38*

**CONTACT:** Dartmouth Outing Club: **outdoors.dartmouth.edu**; Appalachian Mountain Club: **outdoors.org**

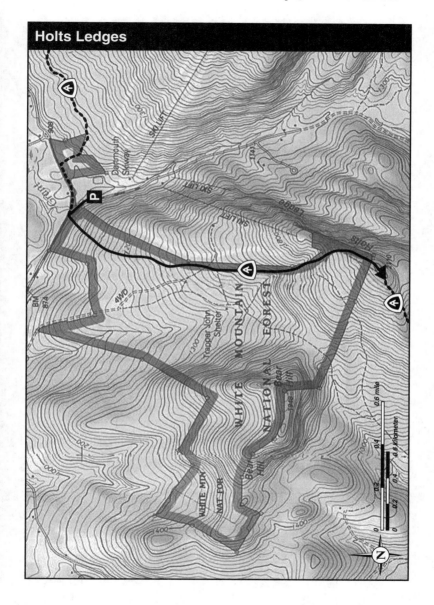

**Holts Ledges**

## Overview

The Holts Ledges hike boasts some impressively steep sections, but the sweeping views of Winslow Ledge and the valley to the south make the hike well worthwhile.

## Route Details

Holts Ledges on the southern side of the Dartmouth Skiway ski area is an impressively steep hike that rewards you with epic views of the valley below. The trail starts right off with a steep climb up a wooden staircase. After that initial lunge, the trail continues its steep initial climb. It's quite a sudden warm-up for the hike. The trail surface is mostly hard-packed dirt punctuated by a few roots running across the trail. At first, the trail winds up toward the left (north), heading toward the ski area. For the first section of the hike, at least 15 minutes in, the trail maintains its steep climb and fairly rough surface underfoot.

On the first section of the hike, you're climbing aggressively over a fairly rough trail surface. It's quite a wake-up call. After that, the trail surface gets smoother, but the trail pitch maintains its sustained, steep climb. The forest here is fairly open at the ground level, with a high forest canopy of mostly birch. The trail takes a circuitous path, winding to the left and right through the forest, all the while maintaining its fairly strenuous climb. The trail is nice and

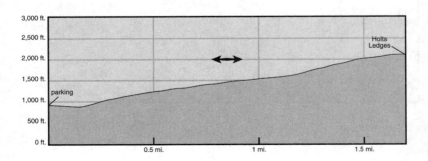

steep, just like the trails on the Holts Ledges side of the Dartmouth Skiway ski area.

The trail surface grows rougher underfoot, with lots of intersecting roots and rocks. Then about 30 minutes into the hike, you'll pass over an old stone wall. Just after that, the trail pitch mellows out slightly for a while but picks up again not long after. Here the trail is still quite rocky and root covered.

The trail continues its steady ascent up the side of the Dartmouth Skiway hill. You can't see any of the ski trails, though, as you are deep in the woods here. As this is a fairly popular trail, it's extremely well-defined and fairly well marked with white blazes. About 45 minutes into the hike, you'll cross over the remnants of another old stone wall, left over from the 1800s when this entire area was cleared for farmland.

The trail character remains consistent—a sustained, steady climb over a fairly rough surface on a twisty, windy path. Portions of the trail can be quite muddy from runoff down the steep slopes. Consequently, it can also be fairly buggy here in the height of summer, so be prepared. This may not be what I would call a kid-friendly hike, but it's good for older kids.

About 40 minutes into the hike, you enter a forest protection zone. After this, it feels as if you're hiking beneath a canopy of young birch and maple. The trail pitch mellows a bit here and the trail surface is smoother, with a blanket of pine needles. Shortly after that, about 45 minutes in, you'll cross over an old fire road bed. Proceed straight across the fire road to the Appalachian Trail (A.T.) on the other side.

After crossing over the old fire road, about 1 hour into the hike, the trail pitch remains slightly mellower. Then you'll come to the intersection with a short spur trail down to the Trapper John A.T. shelter. The shelter is 0.3 mile off the main trail. The trail surface here is also smoother, with a nice soft blanket of pine needles. Shortly after passing the turnoff for the shelter, you'll cross over a small gully and streambed.

Shortly after passing over that streambed, the pitch steepens considerably. The surface here is a bit more washed out because of the steep nature of the trail. After about 50 yards of this steep climb up a rocky and unstable surface, the trail crosses back over the streambed below. It's not quite as steep as that short, straight section, but it continues a sustained, steep climb.

After crossing back over the streambed, the trail surface is quite root covered. Watch your step on these off-angle roots, especially on wet or rainy days. The trail here is also quite well-defined and well marked. After a relatively brief climb up this continued steep section, you'll see a clearing ahead in the trees. There is a huge drop here, so approach with caution. A short stand of shrubs is all that separates you from a drop of a couple hundred feet.

While the view here is dramatic, continue on the right on the A.T. to get to the rest of Holts Ledges. Again, be extremely careful here. The view and the drop-off are equally dramatic. It's tempting to lean out to get a good picture, but don't lean out too far.

## Nearby Attractions

Hanover and Lebanon, New Hampshire, are nearby, which provide numerous cultural, lodging, and dining options. Hanover also has the distinction of being designated an official Appalachian Trail Community.

## Directions

From Lyme, New Hampshire, follow the Grafton Turnpike for slightly more than 3 miles to where Dorchester Road splits off to the left. Just after that, follow the Grafton Turnpike another 100 feet to the right heading toward the ski area. There's plenty of room to park in one of the lower ski area parking lots on the left. The trailhead is located off to the right as you drive in.

# 27

# Smarts Mountain

**YOU'LL COME ACROSS *VIA FERRATA* ON THE HIKE UP SMARTS MOUNTAIN.**

**GPS TRAILHEAD COORDINATES:** N43° 47.829' W72° 4.292'

**DISTANCE & CONFIGURATION:** 7.8-mile out-and-back

**HIKING TIME:** 5.5 hours

**HIGHLIGHTS:** Impressive views from Lambert Ridge

**ELEVATION:** 3,230' at summit, 1,330' at trailhead

**ACCESS:** Parking in dirt lot off Dorchester Road

**MAPS:** Appalachian Trail Conservancy *NH–VT Map 4* and DeLorme *NH Atlas & Gazetteer Map 38*

**CONTACT:** Dartmouth Outing Club: **outdoors.dartmouth.edu**; Appalachian Mountain Club: **outdoors.org**

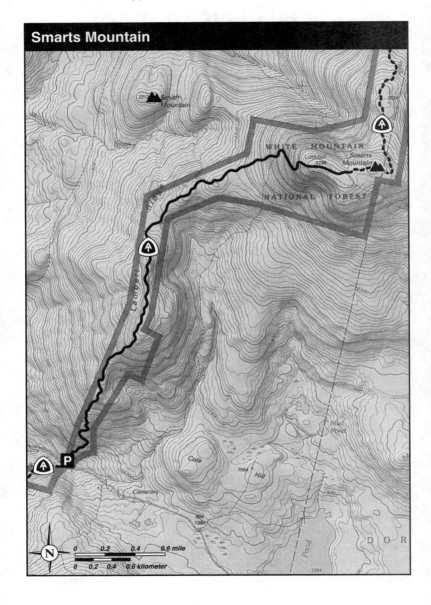

## Smarts Mountain

## Overview

Smarts Mountain is a lengthy hike over the truly scenic Lambert Ridge. Along the way, you'll be treated to sweeping views of the surrounding forests.

## Route Details

There are two trailheads that leave from the Smarts Mountain parking area. Make sure you're on the white-blazed Appalachian Trail (A.T.) and not the other blue-blazed Fire Road–Fire Tower Trail. There's a beautiful stream running by the parking area if you need to water up, but be sure to treat it or run it through a filter. There's space for about 10 cars or so in this dirt area.

The woods here are fairly dense and this is a remote area, so make sure you have the right supplies, including bug repellent. The Lambert Ridge Trail up Smarts Mountain is the A.T. The trail starts out at a moderate grade. You're hiking through a dense, lush forest of mostly maple, birch, and pine. The trail here is fairly well-defined and well marked as it winds its way up the hillside. About 10 minutes into the hike, you'll be scrambling up through a rocky gorge. Keep an eye on the white blazes, as it could be easy to wander off-trail here.

The trail here still has a variable but mostly moderate grade, and it is certainly more well-defined here. The trail surface is mostly pine needles and rocks. Smarts Mountain is a popular hiking destination, so this trail is frequently used and well maintained.

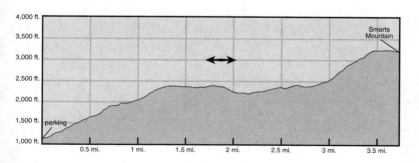

The trail continues its moderate, winding ascent. About 15 minutes in, the pitch increases a bit and you're climbing more aggressively for a good long section. Then after 5 minutes of steeper hiking, the pitch becomes more moderate again as the trail passes over a water runoff. The trail is well-defined here but not all that well marked, so pay attention.

You'll cross over what's left of an old stone wall next at about 25 minutes into the hike. If your heart is starting to pound from the hike, imagine the effort early farmers took to build this stone wall up on the lower flanks of Smarts Mountain. The trail continues its moderate and steady ascent. The trail surface ranges from soft pine needles to roots, rocks, and mud.

Then, at about the 30-minute mark, you'll pass a large rock ledge on the right as the trail switches back to the left. There's a good possibility of bear habitat in these types of multilevel rock ledges. Shortly after passing this rock ledge, the trail switches back to the left and the surface becomes quite rocky. Atop the rock ledge, the trail flattens out somewhat and gives you a break. Immediately following is a brief, swampy section where the route is not that well marked or defined, so watch where you're going.

Then the trail veers to the right and becomes significantly rockier. Ahead of you through the trees, you can see another massive rock ledge. You'll soon be on top of this, after ascending a steep, rocky section. There is a beautiful vista from atop this ledge where the path veers left. You'll realize you've gained some elevation, but you still have quite a ways to go. That view is just the first of many coming up.

As you make your way to the top of Lambert Ridge after about 45 minutes of hiking, you'll come to a dramatic, sweeping view of the backcountry to the north and west and the summit of Smarts Mountain. This view definitely recharges you after the steep, rocky hike it took to get here. As you hike along the top of Lambert Ridge and reenter the woods, breathe in the deep balsam scent of the forest. There's also a nice little rock garden to scramble over as soon as you dive back into the forest. After this, it's a relatively gentle ridgeline ramble as you approach the Smarts Mountain summit.

The forest feels lighter and more open as you hike along Lambert Ridge. You'll be in and out of the woods with more views to either side. At a couple of clearings, there will be some rock cairns to mark the way. After passing through a couple of these clearings, you'll face a moderately steep granite ledge. It can be easy to mistake veins of milky quartz in the rock for white blazes, so pay close attention. After you reenter the woods once again, the trail pitch steepens again.

The trail maintains its steep ascent, and the surface is crossed with many roots and rocks. The route is not too well marked here but quite well-defined. You are definitely gaining altitude on the ridgeline as you approach the summit cone of Smarts Mountain. The trail here is quite dramatic and scenic, with several rock gardens and more clearings as you ascend the ledge. The trail has a few brief descents, but you're mostly climbing as you move along the ridge.

When you're in the woods along the ridge, you're hiking through a verdant pine forest. At 1 hour and 30 minutes, you come to another opening on the ledge. From here, you can see the rest of Lambert Ridge, the summit of Smarts Mountain, and the old fire tower on top. As you reenter the woods off the ledge, you can feel the trail veering to the right for the final lunge up to the summit. Between the ridges, there's a peaceful ramble for a few moments before the trail regains its intensity. After a 30-minute-or-so ramble, the trail pitches upward and you can tell it's going to stay that way.

Once you're truly on the final part of the hike, the trail is steep and rocky. There are a couple of stone staircases to aid your climb. There are several long, smooth granite ledges that are a bit off angle, so be careful with your footing. This section of rock ledges and stone staircases is quite steep and continues for quite a ways, so take your time.

Toward the top of one steep pitch, you'll come to the intersection of the A.T. and the blue-blazed Smarts Ranger Trail. This is about 2 hours and 20 minutes into the hike. The trail is extremely rocky after this intersection, but you will encounter a few stone staircases and some iron bars—known as *via ferrata*, the "iron way"—to help with the climb over the often-wet, slippery granite.

The trail will switch back to the right, then eventually back to the left. The path is steep and rocky as you near the summit, with a couple of spots where you really wouldn't want to fall. So again, take your time and be careful. As the pitch relaxes near the top, the surrounding forest is still fairly dense and mostly conifers. The balsam forest smells like Christmas. It's just short of 3 hours to the top, and you can hang out and relax at an A.T. tent site with dramatic views or the old fire tower before heading back down.

## Nearby Attractions

Hanover and Lebanon, New Hampshire, are nearby, which provide numerous cultural, lodging, and dining options.

## Directions

From I-91, take Exit 14, and turn right onto VT 113 East. In 1.4 miles, turn right onto US 5 and make an immediate left to continue on VT 113 for another 1.8 miles as it turns into East Thetford Road. As you pass through Lyme, New Hampshire, the road becomes Grafton Turnpike–Dorchester Road. Continue on Dorchester Road 2.2 miles after it splits to the left (Grafton Turnpike leads to the right and Dartmouth Skiway). Shortly after the split, the road becomes a dirt road. The parking area will be on the left.

SCENERY: ★ ★ ★ ★
TRAIL CONDITION: ★ ★ ★
CHILDREN: ★ ★ ★
DIFFICULTY: ★ ★ ★
SOLITUDE: ★ ★ ★ ★

**THE GRANITE SUMMIT CAP ON MOUNT CUBE GIVES YOU COMMANDING VIEWS OF THE BACKCOUNTRY.**

**GPS TRAILHEAD COORDINATES:** N43° 54.082' W71° 59.050'

**DISTANCE & CONFIGURATION:** 6.8-mile out-and-back

**HIKING TIME:** 4.66 hours

**HIGHLIGHTS:** Sweeping views from clear summit

**ELEVATION:** 2,909' at summit, 809' at trailhead

**ACCESS:** Parking along NH 25A

**MAPS:** Appalachian Trail Conservancy *NH–VT Map 4* and DeLorme *NH Atlas & Gazetteer Map 38*

**CONTACT:** Dartmouth Outing Club: **outdoors.dartmouth.edu**; Appalachian Mountain Club: **outdoors.org**

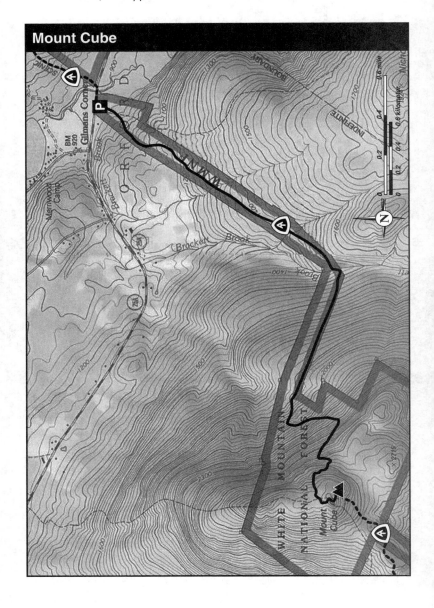

Mount Cube

## Overview

Mount Cube is a nice, rolling, rambling hike with some steep areas toward the top and a clear granite summit that affords spectacular views.

## Route Details

The Mount Cube Trail starts off with a gentle grade and quickly gets you into a dense forest. The trail surface here is a soft bed of pine needles. It can be very buggy in these dense woods, so make sure you've brought your favorite bug stuff. Ten minutes into the hike, you'll pass what looks like a small campsite off to the left. Then the trail crosses over a small stream and an old stone wall. Here the trail starts to ascend a bit more, but the grade is still quite moderate.

The route is very well-defined and well marked here, so it's easy to follow. The trail parallels the path of the stream to the right. Along the stream, the trail gets a bit rockier and steeper. Ten minutes into the hike, you'll pass over another old stone wall. The pitch here is still moderate, but the surface is fairly rocky.

After about 20 minutes, you'll pass over an old fire road. The Appalachian Trail (A.T.) crosses straight over and then descends a bit from the road bed. The trail continues to roll and meander through the dense forest. At 25 minutes into the hike, there's another small stream crossing. The sound of the stream echoing through the forest is quite peaceful as you approach it. After crossing over this stream,

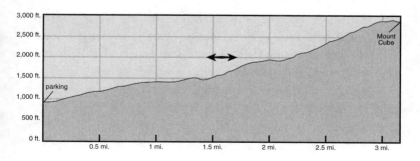

**MANY TRAILS INTERSECT ATOP MOUNT CUBE.**

the trail pitches upward and veers to the left. After a brief, steep climb, the trail returns to its moderate pitch.

There's another, larger stream crossing about 40 minutes into the hike. You pass down through a ravine and over the stream. It's quite scenic. Just after that crossing, the trail pitch increases a bit for a sustained, slightly steeper climb. The trail still has the feel of following along the side of a ridgeline as it leads you closer to Mount Cube. At 50 minutes into the hike, you'll descend a short, steep stone staircase to another spectacularly scenic stream crossing.

On the other side of this crossing, the trail pitches up dramatically and stays that way. You'll come to another set of stone stairs, and the surface will grow a bit more root covered and rocky as you continue to steadily climb. The trail becomes significantly steeper and rockier for about 30 minutes or so of climbing; then it becomes a bit more moderate. You're about 1 hour and 20 minutes in at this point in the hike. You've definitely gained some altitude here, which you can see by looking out through the trees.

For the last hour or so of the hike, the trail continues its moderate to steep ascent. The trail takes a few large, sweeping switchbacks, which get tighter and closer together as you get higher up near the summit. The summit cap is quite rocky, with some large boulders to scramble over to a granite outcrop with spectacular views of the surrounding backcountry. Mount Cube isn't really high enough to be above treeline, yet the summit cap is clear. This is a fairly long hike, and with the exception of the last hour, it's not excessively steep. The views from the top are worth every step, though.

## Nearby Attractions

The last large town you'll likely drive through is Plymouth, New Hampshire, which has plenty of lodging and dining options.

## Directions

From I-91, take Exit 15 in Orford, New Hampshire. Turn left onto US 5 North; in 0.5 mile, turn right onto NH 25A. After crossing the Connecticut River, turn right to stay on NH 25A; in 0.3 mile, turn left again onto NH 25A. In 9.9 miles, you'll see the brown hikers-crossing sign, and you'll know you're almost there. Park on the right (south) side of NH 25A.

Alternatively, take I-93 to Exit 26. Continue onto NH 3A for 4 miles, and veer right onto NH 25 West. In 11.7 miles, in Wentworth, New Hampshire, turn left onto NH 25A, and go 4.5 miles. You'll know you're almost there when you see the brown hikers-crossing sign. Park on the left (south) side of NH 25A.

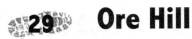 

# 29

# Ore Hill

SCENERY: ★ ★ ★ ★
TRAIL CONDITION: ★ ★ ★
CHILDREN: ★ ★ ★ ★
DIFFICULTY: ★ ★
SOLITUDE: ★ ★ ★ ★

**ORE HILL IS A GREAT HIKE FOR LITTLE KIDS.**

**GPS TRAILHEAD COORDINATES:** N43° 57.014' W71° 56.343'

**DISTANCE & CONFIGURATION:** 1.5-mile out-and-back

**HIKING TIME:** 1.25 hours

**HIGHLIGHTS:** Hike takes you through truly scenic forest

**ELEVATION:** 1,850' at summit, 1,530' at trailhead

**ACCESS:** Park alongside NH 25C

**MAPS:** Appalachian Trail Conservancy *NH–VT Map 4* and DeLorme *NH Atlas & Gazetteer Map 38*

**CONTACT:** Dartmouth Outing Club: **outdoors.dartmouth.edu**; Appalachian Mountain Club: **outdoors.org**

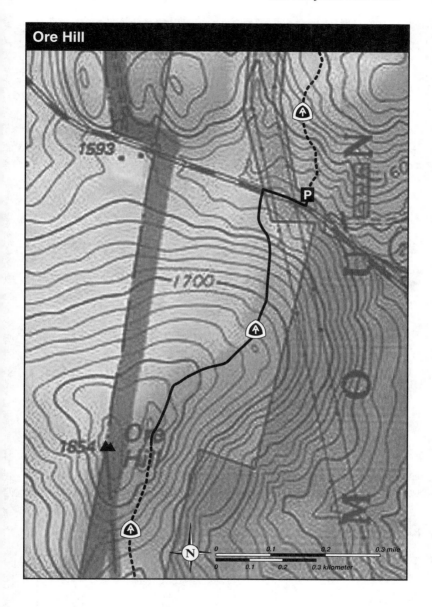

## Overview

This is a fun, kid-friendly hike that feels more remote, but it's really not too far.

## Route Details

Anywhere the Appalachian Trail (A.T.) crosses a road, there's the potential for having two day hikes across from each other. This is the case with Ore Hill and Mount Mist—the trailheads are on either side of NH 25C. This is a nice pair of hikes. Mount Mist is a good hike for kids, but Ore Hill is even better for smaller kids, as it's a shorter and gentler hike overall.

The trailhead for Ore Hill is about 50 yards down NH 25C to the west–northwest from the Mount Mist trailhead. At the start, it parallels a row of power lines. As soon as you get into the woods, the forest around the trail is quite dense.

The trail follows the path of the power lines for a while and takes a short, twisting climb to the right, deeper into the woods. The trail settles into a rhythm similar to that of the Mount Mist Trail on the other side of the road. It's a gentle ramble through the woods instead of an aggressive climb and descent.

The trail twists and winds up through dense undergrowth and lots of young maples trying to match their taller brethren overhead. The trail is narrow and twisting but well-defined and fairly

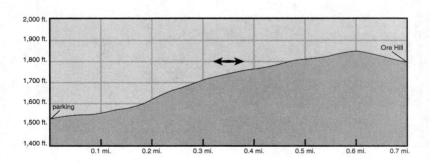

well marked. It's still only at a moderate grade. The winding trail is still generally following a course roughly parallel to the power lines. About 10 minutes into the hike, the trail begins a moderate but steady climb. The trail is still narrow and circuitous here but well-defined and easy to follow.

The forest here is lush and green with lots of ferns and young maple trees blanketing the forest. Keep an eye out for the white blazes as the trail winds through the woods, following a serpentine path. There are a couple of steeper sections here, but they're never too steep, and there's always a gentle rolling section afterward. About 30 minutes into the hike, you'll come to a stone staircase, five large boulders that make up a natural stairway. After that, the trail pitch mellows considerably for a section, though you're still moving through a very dense forest.

There's still a moderate grade to the trail but a steady elevation gain. The surrounding forest and undergrowth is still quite dense as well. The trail surface here is fairly rough, with lots of roots and rocks. So watch your footing and make sure any little kids are doing the same.

The Ore Hill Trail is a bit steeper in the midsection than Mount Mist across the street, but it's still quite a kid-friendly hike. The trail cuts back and forth through the dense forest, making for a very scenic hike. The woods are also cool on hot summer days. The trail continues its moderate yet steady ascent.

The ground cover and higher forest canopy a bit farther into the hike mean the trail is quite well-defined. There's very little risk of wandering off the trail. After a brief, flat stroll through the lush, green forest, the trail pitches up slightly and gets a bit more twisty and windy again.

If you wanted to extend this hike, you could do a 4-mile out-and-back to the Ore Hill shelter. Just doing Ore Hill itself is a great kid's hike. The forest itself is quite scenic and will remind your kids of Winnie-the-Pooh's Hundred Acre Wood. The trail continues its gentle ascent. When you reach the rounded top of Ore Hill, the forest opens up, and you'll realize you've reached the top of this hill.

The trail continues to descend into a small gully, so if you get to that point, you've gone past the summit. It's not a very clear, well-defined summit, like many smaller hikes in New England. There's a small grassy spot here where you could break for lunch or a snack before heading back down or continuing, if you plan to extend the hike.

## Nearby Attractions

The last large town you'll likely drive through is Plymouth, New Hampshire, which has plenty of lodging and dining options.

## Directions

Take I-93 to Exit 26. Continue onto NH 3A for 4 miles, and veer right onto NH 25 West. In 11.7 miles, in Wentworth, New Hampshire, head north on NH 118/NH 25 for 3.9 miles through Warren. Bear left onto NH 25C, and go 3.3 miles. Park along the right side of NH 25C where the A.T. crosses the highway.

# 30

# Mount Mist

SCENERY: ★ ★ ★
TRAIL CONDITION: ★ ★ ★
CHILDREN: ★ ★ ★
DIFFICULTY: ★ ★ ★
SOLITUDE: ★ ★ ★ ★

**THE MOUNT MIST HIKE IS A LONG, GENTLE RAMBLE.**

**GPS TRAILHEAD COORDINATES:** N43° 57.014' W71° 56.343'

**DISTANCE & CONFIGURATION:** 4.8-mile out-and-back

**HIKING TIME:** 2.75 hours

**HIGHLIGHTS:** Gentle ramble through diverse forest

**ELEVATION:** 2,230' at summit, 1,530' at trailhead

**ACCESS:** Park alongside NH 25C

**MAPS:** Appalachian Trail Conservancy *NH–VT Map 4* and DeLorme *NH Atlas & Gazetteer Map 38*

**CONTACT:** Dartmouth Outing Club: **outdoors.dartmouth.edu**; Appalachian Mountain Club: **outdoors.org**

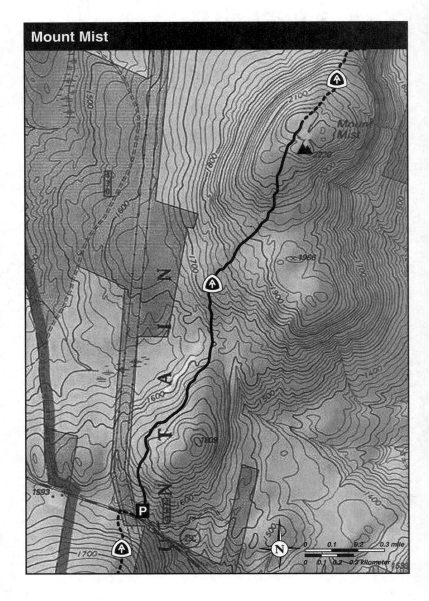

## Overview

The Mount Mist hike is a nice, relatively easy ramble through the forest.

## Route Details

The Mount Mist Trail drops down off the road and over a quiet little stream before continuing into a dense forest. The trail begins as a moderate yet steady climb just after passing over the stream. The trail is fairly well-defined and well marked here. As always, if you feel like you haven't seen a blaze for a while, simply turn around. The trail may be better marked in the other direction.

The trail wends its way along a side hill, with a nice, moderate grade as it slowly climbs. This would also be a fairly good kid-friendly hike. The trail surface is mostly soft pine needles, though there are a few spots where it becomes a bit more root-bound. Just about 10 or 15 minutes into the hike, the trail follows along the path of an old stone wall, then continues rolling up and over through the forest.

The trail rises and falls but is never overly steep. It brings you through a dense forest of birch, maple, and pine. About 20 minutes into the hike, the trail becomes a bit rockier and narrower. The trail is still quite well-defined and easy to follow. The trail continues winding up the hillside at a moderate grade.

Then the trail heads down a bit, seemingly following along the hillside to the east. The Mount Mist hike is very gentle so far, which

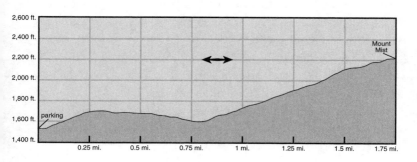

makes it a great hike for kids. The trail surface is still primarily pine needles with some tree roots. The gentle rise and fall of the trail continues, making for a nice, gentle ramble in the woods.

The forest here is still quite dense, which makes it nice and cool on those hot summer days, but it can also be buggy, so bring your favorite bug stuff. About 40 minutes into the hike, the forest canopy begins to loosen, which lets a bit more light into the forest and down to the forest floor. There's a lot of birch in the forest here and more dense undergrowth.

The trail continues, rolling up and down through the dense undergrowth with a loose forest canopy overhead. Then the trail gets quite muddy and root-bound for a stretch. Watch your step here, as the mud can be fairly soupy if it has been raining a lot recently. After this brief muddy section, the trail begins to climb again.

The trail is climbing steadily here, but it's still a moderate grade—never too steep. After about 45 minutes into the hike, the trail is still skirting along a hillside through the dense forest. It's a peaceful and relaxing hike. You've steadily been hiking away from the road, so it's very quiet in here. After about 1 hour of hiking, you cross an old fire roadbed. Simply cross directly over the old roadbed to stay on the Appalachian Trail (A.T.).

The trail becomes a bit more dense and winding after passing over this roadbed. Keep an eye out for the white blazes, as it would be a bit easier to wander off-trail here. There's always a relaxed sigh after seeing a blaze for the first time in a while. The trail here is fairly well-defined but not all that well marked. There are a lot of birch trees here and older trees with the bark peeling off, so some of the blazes may have become obscured.

The trail may not be that well marked but continues to be well-defined and well trodden. Hike slowly and pay attention to the trail itself. About 1 hour and 30 minutes into the hike, persevere and you'll make it through the relatively unmarked section to the summit at an elevation of 2,230 feet.

At the summit of Mount Mist, there's a small clearing and a faded wooden sign with the name and elevation carved into it. This is a great spot for lunch or a quick break before heading down. The long, rambling nature of the hike and the fact that it's never excessively steep make this an excellent hike for kids.

## Nearby Attractions

The last large town you'll likely drive through is Plymouth, New Hampshire, which has plenty of lodging and dining options.

## Directions

Take I-93 to Exit 26. Continue onto NH 3A for 4 miles, and veer right onto NH 25 West. In 11.7 miles, in Wentworth, New Hampshire, head north on NH 118/NH 25 for 3.9 miles through Warren. Bear left onto NH 25C, and go 3.3 miles. Park along the right side of NH 25C where the A.T. crosses the highway.

# Townline Trail

SCENERY: ★ ★ ★ ★
TRAIL CONDITION: ★ ★ ★
CHILDREN: ★ ★ ★
DIFFICULTY: ★ ★ ★
SOLITUDE: ★ ★ ★ ★

**FOR THE MOST PART, TOWNLINE TRAIL IS A RELAXING STROLL THROUGH THE FOREST.**

**GPS TRAILHEAD COORDINATES:**
N43° 59.397' W71° 53.974'

**DISTANCE & CONFIGURATION:** 2.8-mile out-and-back

**HIKING TIME:** 1 hour

**HIGHLIGHTS:** Jeffers Brook

**ELEVATION:** 1,375' at trail end, 1,250' at trailhead

**ACCESS:** Large parking area on western side of NH 25

**MAPS:** Appalachian Trail Conservancy *NH–VT Map 4* and DeLorme *NH Atlas & Gazetteer Map 42*

**CONTACT:** Dartmouth Outing Club: **outdoors.dartmouth.edu**; Appalachian Mountain Club: **outdoors.org**

## Townline Trail

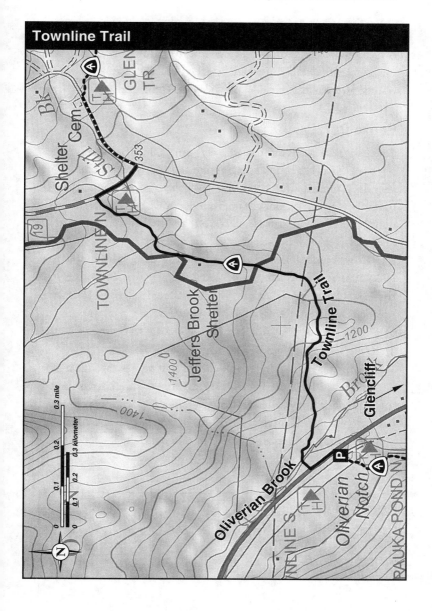

## Overview

A nice ramble up and over a ridgeline with a pristine stream flowing by near the end. You could also start for Moosilauke here if you wanted to make that already long hike even longer.

## Route Details

Townline Trail starts off immediately with a fairly wide stream crossing over Oliverian Brook and through the Oliverian Notch. It's not very deep, but it's wide. Often you'll be able to hop from rock to rock, but if there has been a lot of rain, your feet might get wet. Bring a pair of water sandals, just in case. Plus, you can use them at the end of the hike and wade into the stream near the end.

The Townline Trail leads to the Glencliff Trail up Mount Moosilauke. The Townline Trail would add 1.4 miles in either direction to the Moosilauke hike. Overall, the Townline Trail is a nice ramble through the forest, though it does have a few steep sections. It would be a good warm-up for Moosilauke if you were to combine the two. That combination would be an exceptionally long hike.

The trail is quite well-defined here as it passes through a fairly dense forest. After crossing over the stream, the trail heads directly into the forest away from NH 25. After about 15 minutes or so, you begin to climb a relatively short, steep ridgeline. You'll come to a stone staircase at the start of this climb. This is really the only steeper

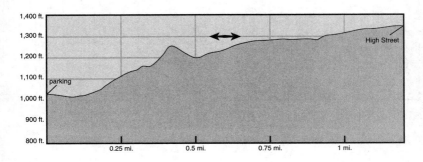

section on the Townline Trail, so this is quite a good hike if you have the kids in tow. After that short climb up the hillside, the trail continues its gentle roll through the forest.

About 30 minutes into the Townline Trail, you'll come to a footbridge over a stream. To the left is the Jeffers Brook campsite, a beautiful brookside camping spot. This would be a great place to spend the night camping with your kids. Off to the right of the trail is Jeffers Brook, which is a spectacularly scenic brook. This is a perfect place to relax on the rocks or wade into the brook on a hot day.

Just past the Jeffers Brook campsite, you'll come to the end of the Townline Trail. There's a small parking area for about five cars or so. This could be an alternate place to park if you didn't want to deal with crossing NH 25 or doing the longer stream crossing at the other end of the Townline Trail. Head out to the paved road and hike 0.3 mile up to the Glencliff trailhead if your plan is to continue up Moosilauke.

Just doing the Townline Trail is 1 hour either way. The gentle grade, the beautiful Jeffers Brook, and the relative short distance all make this an excellent choice for a day hike with the kids.

## Nearby Attractions

The last large town you'll likely drive through is Plymouth, New Hampshire, which has plenty of lodging and dining options.

## Directions

Take I-93 to Exit 26. Continue onto NH 3A for 4 miles, and veer right onto NH 25 West. Follow NH 25 for a total of 20.7 miles through Wentworth, Warren, and finally Glencliff, New Hampshire. Parking will be on the left (west) side of NH 25.

SCENERY: ★ ★ ★ ★ ★
TRAIL CONDITION: ★ ★ ★
CHILDREN: ★ ★
DIFFICULTY: ★ ★ ★ ★
SOLITUDE: ★ ★ ★

**THE SUMMIT OF MOUNT MOOSILAUKE IS A WELCOME SIGHT AFTER A LONG, ARDUOUS HIKE.**

**GPS TRAILHEAD COORDINATES:** N43° 59.915' W71° 52.887'

**DISTANCE & CONFIGURATION:** 7.8-mile out-and-back

**HIKING TIME:** 7 hours

**HIGHLIGHTS:** Sweeping views from summit

**ELEVATION:** 4,802' at summit, 2,327' at trailhead

**ACCESS:** Trailhead parking off Glencliff Road

**MAPS:** Appalachian Trail Conservancy *NH–VT Map 4* and DeLorme *NH Atlas & Gazetteer Map 43*

**CONTACT:** Dartmouth Outing Club: **outdoors.dartmouth.edu**; Appalachian Mountain Club: **outdoors.org**

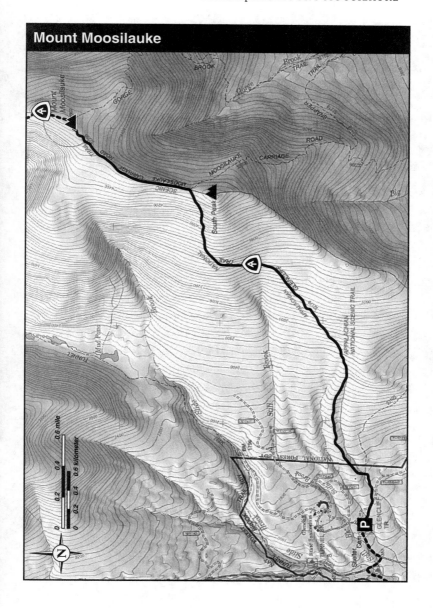

## Overview

Mount Moosilauke is a popular, long, and strenuous hike, but it is definitely worth every step when you see the 360-degree views from the summit.

## Route Details

The Glencliff Trail up Mount Moosilauke is a popular hiking route. Consequently, it's quite well marked and well-defined. Shortly after starting the hike, there's a brief stream crossing. Then the trail begins a steady, moderate ascent through a dense forest. At about 5 minutes into the hike, you'll pass the first of several open fields; this one you'll see through the woods to the right of the trail.

Shortly after passing that open field, the trail overlaps with a fire road. The fire road then takes you past several other open fields on both sides of the trail. The second one is quite expansive and lined with apple trees. The third field is the largest. The fire road and trail follow along the left side of the field. Then when the trail reenters the woods, you have 3.7 miles to the summit of Mount Moosilauke. At this intersection and stream crossing, the Appalachian Trail (A.T.) goes straight ahead while the Dartmouth Outing Club Carriage Trail heads off to the right.

The pitch increases about 30 minutes into the hike, just after that intersection. It's relatively moderate for most of the first couple of hours of the hike. Later, about 50 minutes into the hike, the trail

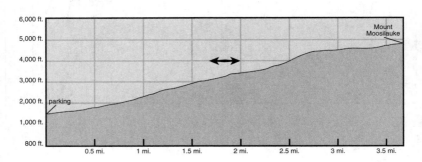

follows along the course of a stream. It also gets slightly steeper here and starts to take some moderate switchbacks. At 1 hour in, you'll cross a stream over a small footbridge. After this bridge, the surface grows much rockier.

The lush scent of the forest is heavy in the air here. The route is still quite well-defined and well marked, and it maintains its steady, moderate climb. The surface is firm, punctuated by roots and rocks. It's also quite well maintained, as you'll encounter several water bars put in place by trail crews to minimize erosion. Then the trail takes you on a series of switchbacks.

The trail now has a steep to moderate pitch and follows a series of switchbacks. The forest here is a bit less dense and slightly more open overhead, which lets some light into the forest. Then the trail veers to the left as if following along a ridgeline. The path wanders back into denser forest. At 1 hour and 45 minutes into the hike, there's another fairly significant stream crossing. After crossing over, the trail takes you through a nice, open glade.

There's an almost junglelike quality to the forest here, with the moss-covered rocks and dense, low forest on either side of the trail. The rocky trail is still taking you on a steady ascent. After ascending a short, steep stone staircase, the trail steepens again. At just short of 2 hours into the hike, you are in a steady, steep, rocky area. There are numerous trail maintenance features like water bars and the stone staircases.

Past the 2-hour mark into the hike, the trail by now is quite rocky and technical. Watch your footing here, as it would be relatively easy to slip or twist an ankle. The last section just below the south peak is exceptionally rocky and steep. This part is tough going both on the way up and down. There are a few tight switchbacks in this section as well. Keep an eye out for the white blazes, as the trail is less well-defined here.

At 3 hours and 30 minutes into the hike, you'll finally emerge from that seemingly incessant steep, rocky climb to another intersection with Carriage Trail that veered off to the right 3.7 miles ago.

From here, a 0.1-mile spur trail leads to the south peak. Continue 0.8 mile to the summit of Moosilauke at its 4,802-foot elevation.

The final push to the summit is much less steep, and you can see the summit the entire time as you approach. Once you're out of the forest, the trail is marked with huge rock cairns, though it's also quite well-defined, so there's very little chance of wandering off the trail. There are several rock walls built atop Mount Moosilauke at which you can sit and block the wind if the wind is up.

Another option is to do the A.T. on the northwestern side of Moosilauke on the Beaver Brook Trail. This is shorter and much steeper, and you'll encounter a lot of *via ferrata,* or the "iron way." These are a series of iron bars hammered into the rock where you would otherwise need climbing gear to ascend a particular section.

Overall, the hike to the summit of Moosilauke is long and strenuous but rewards you with sweeping, panoramic views of the central New Hampshire countryside.

## Nearby Attractions

The last large town you'll likely drive through is Plymouth, New Hampshire, which has plenty of lodging and dining options.

## Directions

Take I-93 to Exit 26. Continue onto NH 3A for 4 miles, and veer right onto NH 25 West. Follow NH 25 for a total of 20.1 miles through Wentworth, Warren, and finally Glencliff, New Hampshire. Turn right onto High Street (following signs for Glencliff Home). Trailhead parking will be just past the trailhead on the right (east) side of the road.

SCENERY: ★ ★ ★ ★ ★
TRAIL CONDITION: ★ ★ ★
CHILDREN: ★ ★ ★
DIFFICULTY: ★ ★ ★ ★
SOLITUDE: ★ ★ ★

**PICTURE-PERFECT VIEWS FROM CASCADE BROOK TRAIL**

**GPS TRAILHEAD COORDINATES:** N44° 5.873' W71° 40.893'

**DISTANCE & CONFIGURATION:** 7.4-mile out-and-back

**HIKING TIME:** 4.5 hours

**HIGHLIGHTS:** Beautiful stream crossings

**ELEVATION:** 2,750' at summit, 1,950' at trailhead

**ACCESS:** Plenty of parking at the Flume Gorge and Visitor Center

**MAPS:** Appalachian Trail Conservancy *NH–VT Map 3* and DeLorme *NH Atlas & Gazetteer Map 43*

**CONTACT:** White Mountain National Forest: **www.fs.usda.gov/whitemountain**

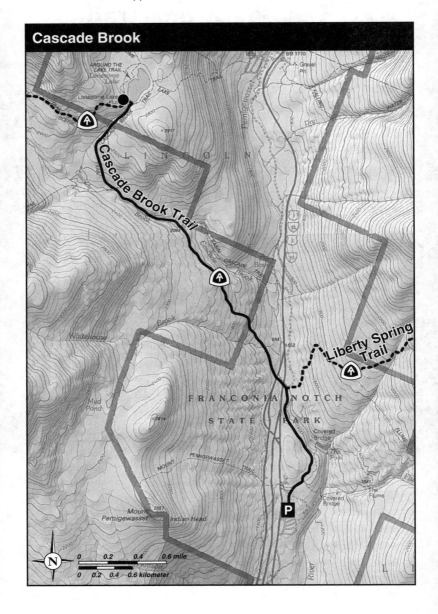

## Overview

Cascade Brook Trail is spectacularly scenic, crossing over the brook, looking east toward the White Mountains, and finally arriving at the placid Lonesome Lake.

## Route Details

Cascade Brook Trail in the southern end of Franconia Notch State Park is a relatively long and spectacularly scenic hike, with dramatic stream and rock crossings and views across the notch to Mount Liberty. You'll park in the Flume Gorge and Visitor Center parking area off US 3 (Exit 34A off I-93). This is an extremely popular tourist spot, but there's plenty of parking, so it shouldn't be a problem. You'll use the same parking spot for Cascade Brook and Mount Liberty.

From the Flume Gorge parking area, there's a short, blue-blazed spur trail (0.8 mile) that leads toward the Pemigewasset River and a paved bike and walking path to the split where Cascade Brook Trail goes to the west and Mount Liberty Trail goes east. This spur trail is a nice warm-up for either hike ahead.

After 20 minutes on the spur trail and the paved bike path, you'll come to a large bridge over the Pemigewasset. This is where you start on the Cascade Brook Trail in earnest. Head down to the left just before the bridge to follow the Cascade Brook Trail. From here, you have 2.9 miles to the Lonesome Lake hut.

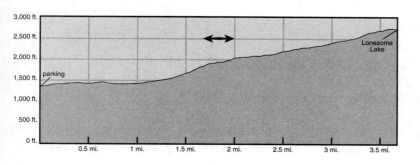

You'll pass under the roadways of the Franconia Notch Parkway as you hike along the Pemigewasset River. After you've crossed under both the northbound and southbound sides, you'll reenter the woods. Here's where the hike truly begins, even though you started off 30 minutes ago. Back in the woods, the trail surface is hard-packed dirt with a few rocks poking through. The trail starts off at a steady but moderate grade. Soon after you enter the woods, you'll come to a small stream crossing and a huge boulder on the left. The trail pitches up here somewhat but remains fairly moderate.

As you continue toward Lonesome Lake, you'll go over a couple more stream crossings. Then 40 minutes in, you'll come to a major stream crossing over Whitehouse Brook, hopping from boulder to boulder. It is truly scenic and spectacular, but take your time and step carefully. You would not want to slip and fall in here. After this crossing, head upstream a bit on the larger rocks and look for the white blaze.

After crossing over Whitehouse Brook, the trail pitch increases and the trail gets steeper and rockier. It's still not too steep though. The trail is well-defined and relatively smooth here. It passes through the undergrowth of a lot of young trees and a high forest canopy of mostly birch and maple. The trail maintains its steady, moderate climb. Then at about 55 minutes in, you'll come to another stream crossing and a large rock garden.

The trail here takes you on a steady yet fairly moderate ascent with a few steeper sections here and there. About 1 hour in, the trail starts becoming rockier and slightly steeper. Looking east through the trees, you can see you're getting higher and deeper into the woods. The trail is heading mostly west and north toward Lonesome Lake. The sound of I-93 has been replaced by the sounds of the wind in the trees and streams rushing by.

You'll come to another major stream crossing at slightly more than 1 hour and 30 minutes into the hike. This is Cascade Brook, for which the trail is named. There's an elaborate rock garden to step around and over. Most of the rocks will be wet, so exercise caution here.

Also keep an eye on the blazes, so you don't wander off the trail. This is a popular hike, so you'll likely have some company while you're here.

Once you've crossed over the stream, the trail continues to maintain a steady, moderate ascent. Here the trail follows along the same course as Cascade Brook, with a couple of steep sections as well. As the trail veers away from the path of the stream, it gets consistently steeper and rockier. You'll cross over a couple of Appalachian Trail footbridges as well.

The last mile is the steepest and rockiest. You'll come to a sign at a trail intersection that marks 0.8 mile to Lonesome Lake. Here the forest opens up to let a lot more light down to the forest floor. The trail is well-defined here but most definitely steeper and rockier.

You'll know you're getting close to Lonesome Lake as the trail gets even steeper and rockier still. At 2 hours and 25 minutes into the hike, you'll pass through a dramatic-looking rock garden. The trail here looks like a rock waterfall. It makes for fairly technical hiking, but the trail itself is quite scenic. Just take your time and watch your step.

Continuing up the Cascade Brook Trail, you'll come out of the woods to a dramatic view of Lonesome Lake and the peak behind it. Then you'll know you've made it. On a hot day, you can take a dip in the lake before heading back down. You can also relax in the Lonesome Lake hut.

## Nearby Attractions

Franconia Notch State Park is full of epic hiking, camping, and biking, plus Echo Lake over closer to Cannon Mountain. You can also ride the Cannon Mountain Aerial Tramway when that's open.

## Directions

Follow I-93 North into Franconia Notch State Park. Take Exit 34A, and follow US 3 South 0.5 mile to the Flume Gorge and Visitor Center parking area.

**Mount Liberty**

**LOOKING NORTH INTO FRANCONIA NOTCH FROM ATOP MOUNT LIBERTY**

**GPS TRAILHEAD COORDINATES:** N44° 5.873' W71° 40.893'

**DISTANCE & CONFIGURATION:** 6.8-mile out-and-back

**HIKING TIME:** 5.25 hours

**HIGHLIGHTS:** Dramatic views from summit

**ELEVATION:** 4,260' at summit, 1,950' at trailhead

**ACCESS:** Plenty of parking at the Flume Gorge and Visitor Center

**MAPS:** Appalachian Trail Conservancy *NH–VT Map 3* and DeLorme *NH Atlas & Gazetteer Map 43*

**CONTACT:** White Mountain National Forest: **www.fs.usda.gov/whitemountain**

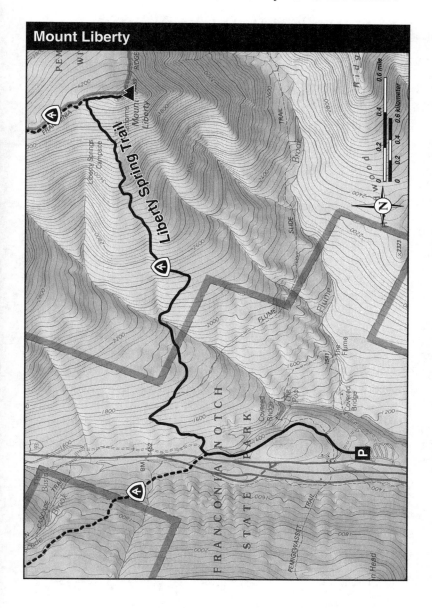

Mount Liberty

## Overview

Mount Liberty is a challenging hike, especially the last two-thirds of the hike up a sustained rocky surface, but you're rewarded with dramatic views of the Franconia Ridge and the Notch.

## Route Details

Mount Liberty is the southernmost of the 4,000-footers that comprise the Franconia Range. From the summit, you can look north along the ridge over the summits of Little Haystack and Mount Lincoln to the dramatic summit of Mount Lafayette. You'll use the same parking area for Cascade Brook and Liberty Springs Trails. Follow the short blue-blazed spur trail to the paved bike path, then follow the bike path and cross the bridge over Pemigewasset River.

Liberty Springs Trail starts out flat for just 50 feet or so, then begins an aggressive, steady climb. The surface is covered with roots and rocks. The steep to moderate ascent continues; at 15 minutes or so, you'll come to the first stone staircase—the first of many.

The trail here heads to the left (north) instead of east, which would be straight up to the peak of Mount Liberty. The trail maintains its sustained, moderate ascent and its rocky and root-bound surface. Looking through the loose forest canopy behind you, you can see the mountains on the west side of Franconia Notch, which is quite a dramatic sight. After 20 minutes, you'll pass a large boulder on the right. The trail continues, following along the ridgeline.

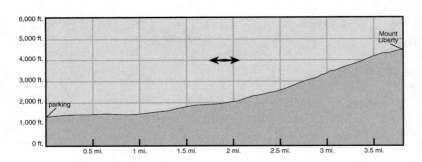

At almost 30 minutes into the hike, you'll come to a stream crossing and another staircase with a couple of loosely spaced stone stairs. Then the trail makes its first switchback to the right as it continues the sustained, steady climb. Now you're hiking through a moderately dense mixed forest of maple, birch, and conifers. After 35 minutes, you'll come to an intersection where the trail splits. The Appalachian Trail (A.T.) and Liberty Springs Trail go off to the left, and Flume Slide Trail goes to the right. The path has become narrower but is still quite rocky and is still maintaining a steady, moderate ascent.

Liberty Springs Trail—and indeed most of the trails within Franconia Notch State Park—is a popular hiking destination, so you will almost certainly have some company on the trail. Also, its popularity helps keep it well-defined, and trail crews keep it well maintained and well marked.

At about the 45-minute mark, you'll round a corner where the trail is heading more to the east. You can see Mount Liberty looming ahead through the trees. The trail pitch is quite gentle in this section. You can consider this a rest before the steeper slopes of Mount Liberty. After another stream crossing, the trail again becomes rockier and begins to climb again. Shortly thereafter, the trail narrows as it follows the course of the stream.

After about 55 minutes, you'll come to another stream crossing. This stream is wide, but there are plenty of rocks to move across without getting wet. It can, of course, be wet and slippery, so be cautious. Right after that stream crossing, you'll come to another stone staircase. Then there are two smaller stream crossings after that. After another stone staircase, the pitch increases and the surface gets rockier. It will be that way for the rest of the hike.

After 1 hour in, you're now truly climbing up the side of Mount Liberty. The trail is consistently steep, and you are climbing on and around large rocks that comprise the trail. The trail itself looks like a rock waterfall for most of the latter two-thirds of the hike. They don't call New Hampshire the Granite State for nothing.

Shortly after the first-hour mark, you'll pass through a rock garden of moss-covered boulders.

It could be easier to lose the trail here, so keep an eye out for the white blazes. After you pass that boulder garden, the trail pitch relaxes slightly and only briefly. Then the trail pitch picks right back up; the trail again gets rockier and slowly switches back to the left (north).

As you continue climbing on this sustained, steep, and rocky trail, the forest mix starts to change to more conifers. Also, as you earn more altitude, the forest becomes denser and lines the sides of the trail, which means the trail here is quite well-defined for most of the hike. After about 1 hour and 20 minutes, you'll ascend an extremely steep and rocky pitch that lasts for more than 100 yards. Your heart will be pumping after that.

Then the trail veers to the right (east) and realigns with the stream cascading down on the left side of the trail. The trail continues its sustained, steep, and rocky ascent. The trail character remains essentially the same for the last 2 hours (or two-thirds) of the hike. As you get higher, the trail switches back several times. You're almost 2 hours into the hike at this point.

After 2 hours and 20 minutes, you'll pass the Liberty Springs tent sites on the left. These tent sites are situated on wooden platforms down off the trail. From here, you're 0.3 mile from the Franconia Ridge Trail that follows the high ridgeline from the summit of Mount Liberty over Little Haystack, Mount Lincoln, and all the way up to Mount Lafayette.

When you reach the Franconia Ridge Trail, that and the A.T. head off to the left. You've come all this way, so you have to head right to summit Mount Liberty. You'll hike over and through some dramatic rock formations up to the granite ridge and rocky summit of Mount Liberty. The views of Franconia Notch and north along the Franconia Ridge Trail to Mount Lafayette are indeed impressive.

YOU'LL FOLLOW A STREAM FOR PART OF THE MOUNT LIBERTY HIKE.

## Nearby Attractions

Franconia Notch State Park is full of epic hiking, camping, and biking, plus Echo Lake over closer to Cannon Mountain. You can also ride the Cannon Mountain Aerial Tramway when it's open.

## Directions

Follow I-93 North into Franconia Notch State Park. Take Exit 34A, and follow US 3 South 0.5 mile to the Flume Gorge and Visitor Center parking area.

SCENERY: ★ ★ ★ ★
TRAIL CONDITION: ★ ★ ★
CHILDREN: ★ ★ ★ ★
DIFFICULTY: ★ ★
SOLITUDE: ★ ★ ★ ★

**RATTLE RIVER TRAIL IS ANOTHER GREAT HIKE FOR YOUNGER KIDS.**

**GPS TRAILHEAD COORDINATES:** N44° 24.070' W71° 6.565'

**DISTANCE & CONFIGURATION:** 3.2-mile out-and-back

**HIKING TIME:** 1.25 hours

**HIGHLIGHTS:** Views of Rattle River

**ELEVATION:** 1,350' at end of trail, 1,250' at trailhead

**ACCESS:** Plenty of parking at trailhead off US 2

**MAPS:** Appalachian Trail Conservancy *NH–VT Map 2* and DeLorme *NH Atlas & Gazetteer Map 49*

**CONTACT:** White Mountain National Forest: **www.fs.usda.gov/whitemountain**

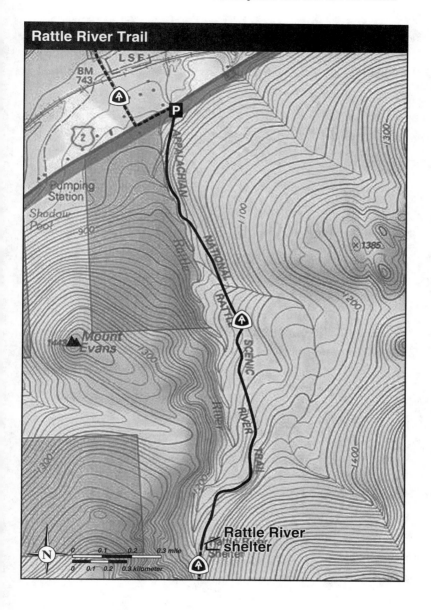

## Rattle River Trail

Rattle River shelter

## Overview

The hike to the Rattle River shelter is a nice, gentle ramble through the forest along the shores of the beautiful Rattle River. This one is perfect for younger kids.

## Route Details

Rattle River Trail is a perfect hike for smaller kids. There's a fairly large trailhead parking area off US 2 in Shelburne on the right (south) just east of Gorham. The trailhead leads right off from the parking lot. From there, it's 1.6 miles to the Rattle River shelter. The wide, gentle trail rambles through a mixed forest of maples, birch, and conifers. The trail is quite well-defined and well marked and follows a gentle to moderate ascent as it winds through the forest.

For the most part, certainly at the beginning, the trail follows the course of the Rattle River off to the right of the trail. You can hear the sound of the rushing water as you're hiking. It's quite relaxing and peaceful. As you're hiking along the gentle trail, there are several spots that are good to just sit and watch the river flowing by.

The trail remains wide and well-defined. You're still hiking through a loosely spaced mixed forest. There don't seem to be too many white blazes marking the trail, but, truth be told, it's so well-defined you don't need them.

About 10 minutes into the hike, a short side trail leads down to the banks of Rattle River. This is one of the first of many spots that

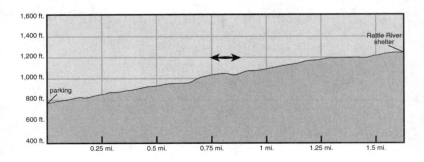

are ideal for a quick break to watch the river. After that, the trail continues its leisurely path through the forest. After a few more minutes, you'll come to another excellent river-viewing spot.

A few minutes past those river vistas, you'll come to a large footbridge over the river. This, too, is a great spot to check out the river and take some pictures looking both upstream and downstream. From where the bridge crosses the river, the Appalachian Trail leads off to the left, veering slightly away from the river. Here the trail becomes slightly narrower, rockier, and a bit steeper. It's still a gentle, kid-friendly grade though.

At about 20 minutes into the hike, you'll come to a small stream crossing—a stream that no doubt feeds into Rattle River. The large, flat rocks make it a simple crossing. After that, the trail continues its gentle ascent into the woods, enshrouded on either side by groves of young conifers.

The trail here is still quite well-defined, if not all that well marked, but again there is little risk of losing the trail or wandering off. A bit farther down, the trail rejoins the course of Rattle River and continues the gentle, rambling ascent. If you have some older kids with you or anyone else who might be interested in a longer hike, they can continue on to Middle Moriah, which would make a nice, long day hike.

Farther along, at about the 40-minute mark, the trail does become a bit rockier and more root-bound. The path still follows the river, which is flowing down and off to the right. Shortly after this section, you will emerge at the Rattle River shelter. From here, a short spur trail leads down to the banks of Rattle River. There are also a few tent sites and an outhouse if you need one. Have lunch here in the shelter and head back, relax down by the river, or continue on for a longer hike to Middle Moriah.

## Nearby Attractions

North Conway, New Hampshire, is south of the Rattle River Trailhead, with numerous lodging and dining options. Mount Washington and the Great Glen Trails are also nearby, as well as camping at the Dolly Copp National Forest campground.

## Directions

From I-93, take Exit 40. Follow US 302 East for 10.8 miles, and turn left onto US 3 North. In 1.8 miles, turn right onto NH 115 North, and go 9.7 miles. Turn right onto US 2 East and go 12.5 miles to Gorham, New Hampshire. Turn right to continue on US 2 for another 4.9 miles; just east of Shelburne, the trailhead parking will be on the right (south side of US 2).

OPPOSITE: RATTLE RIVER IS SPECTACULARLY SCENIC AND PEACEFUL.

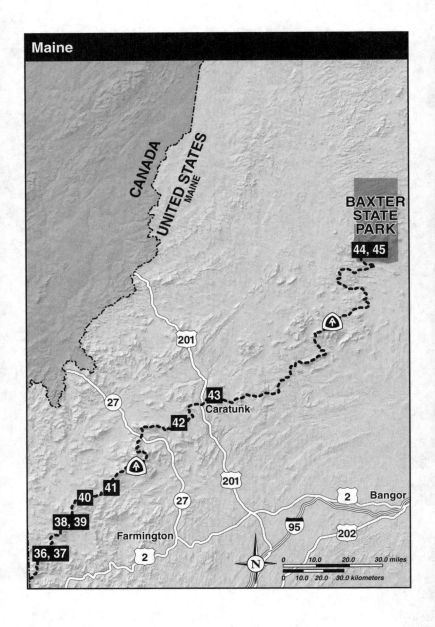

# **Maine**

**THE TRAILHEAD FOR THE MOODY MOUNTAIN HIKE WILL GET YOU WET.**
*(See page 225.)*

**THE FOREST DRAMATICALLY CHANGES CHARACTER OVER THE COURSE OF THE OLD SPECK HIKE.**

**GPS TRAILHEAD COORDINATES:** N44° 35.416' W70° 56.783'

**DISTANCE & CONFIGURATION:** 7.6-mile out-and-back

**HIKING TIME:** 4.75 hours

**HIGHLIGHTS:** Spectacular cliff and waterfall views

**ELEVATION:** 4,180' at summit, 1,110' at trailhead

**ACCESS:** $3 parking fee at ME 26 parking area

**MAPS:** Appalachian Trail Conservancy *ME Map 7* and DeLorme *ME Atlas & Gazetteer Map 18*

**CONTACT:** Maine Department of Agriculture, Conservation and Forestry: **maine.gov/dacf**

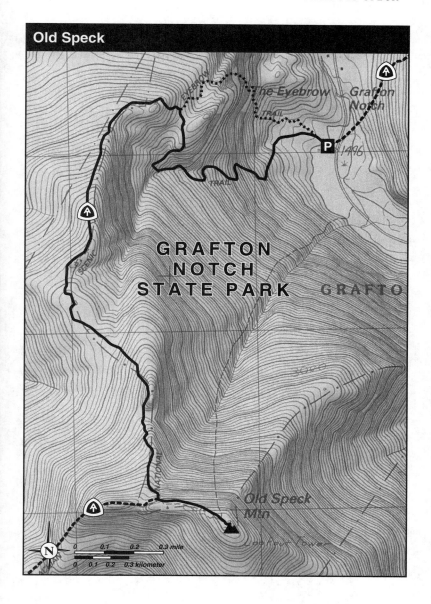

**Old Speck**

The Eyebrow

Grafton Notch

GRAFTON NOTCH STATE PARK

GRAFTO

Old Speck Mtn

0   0.1   0.2   0.3 mile
0   0.1   0.2   0.3 kilometer

## Overview

Old Speck is a strenuous but scenic hike. As Maine's third-highest mountain, Old Speck will treat you to sweeping views of the Mahoosuc Range on the way up and down.

## Route Details

As you prepare for the hike up Old Speck, you will see this forbidding cliff wall ahead of you through the woods. You know that one way or the other, you'll soon be climbing up and around that.

The trailhead for Old Speck leads right out of the parking area on ME 26. There's no need to cross the road as there is to reach the Baldpate trailhead. The trail leads off to the left of the map-and-information kiosk. From there, it's 3.8 miles to the summit. As soon as you enter the woods, the twisting, narrow trail starts climbing right away over a fairly rocky surface.

Shortly into the trail, there's a major stream crossing. There are plenty of rocks piled up in the middle, so rock-hopping your way across is pretty easy. There's little chance of soaking a foot, which would be unfortunate this early in the hike. After the stream crossing, there's a short, steep stone staircase, and the trail pitch picks up considerably and stays that way.

You still have dramatic views of Eyebrow Cliff ahead of you and the western flank of Baldpate across the street. The trail is quite rocky,

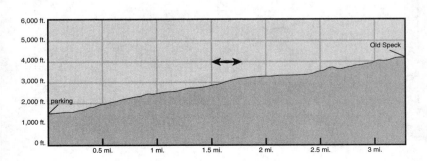

and you will go over several small stream crossings. There's also a consistently steeper pitch here. About 15 minutes into the hike, the trail makes a wide switchback to the right and maintains a steady ascent. You'll come to an Appalachian Trail (A.T.) footbridge that takes you over a steep, moss-covered granite slab. The steady, steep climb then takes you over another set of stone stairs. To the right here, you'll get your first view of the larger stream cascading down the rocks to the right of the trail.

A bit farther up, you'll climb another set of stone stairs, and the trail will pass that cascading stream again, though now it's down lower off the trail. It's quite a dramatic view, and even when it has been fairly dry, the waterfalls are spectacular. After yet another set of stone stairs, the trail takes you through a dramatic grove of conifers. At about 35 minutes in, the trail then veers away from the stream and falls.

Next, you'll come to a log staircase, which is a neat trail feature. The trail continues its steep, steady, rocky climb. You'll pass over some loose rocks and some open granite slabs, all of which can be slick when they're wet, so watch your footing. Now the trail is bringing you through a dramatic forest of tall conifers that forms a dense canopy. The route is certainly well-defined here, though not all that well marked.

At about the 45-minute mark, the trail realigns with that larger stream off to the right as you're heading up. You'll go over a small stream crossing, another stream that feeds into the larger one cascading down the rocks. It's quite a sight. A few minutes later, you'll pass through a clearing that gives you great views of the eastern slopes of Old Speck. Moving over an open rock ledge, the trail then switches back to the left.

The trail winds its way through a small field of boulders. The trail surface is quite root covered here, so step carefully. At 55 minutes into the hike, you'll come out onto an open rock ledge with some spectacular views. Be extremely careful here. A fall here would be disastrous. It can also be easy to lose the trail here, so take the high route away from the cliff edge and you'll find the white blazes again.

At about 1 hour into the hike, the Eyebrow Trail rejoins the A.T. Here the trail pitch is slightly more moderate, but the trail surface is quite rugged with lots of rocks and roots. Shortly after that trail intersection, the trail begins to climb more steeply, still over a rocky surface. Then the trail winds dramatically over roots and rocks through a short, dense forest of scrubby pines. You definitely get the sense that you are at a higher altitude here.

At the 1-hour-and-15-minute mark, the trail crests a small rise. The forest is a bit looser up here, giving you views of the Baldpate Mountain peaks across the street and some of the other surrounding mountains. Then the trail dives back into the forest again. The trail character is still quite rugged, with lots of roots and rocks and extremely steep sections.

In the second hour of the hike, after the Eyebrow Trail intersection, the trail follows a mostly moderate pitch with several intense, steep sections. The trail surface up on this part of the mountain is quite rocky and root covered. This can make for treacherous footing, especially if has been raining recently.

After that first small peak, you feel as if you're following along a ridgeline leading up to the final peak. At 1 hour and 45 minutes, the trail gets consistently steeper. The trail surface is still rocky and uneven, which makes the trail quite well-defined.

After 2 hours and 15 minutes of hiking, the trail crests up and over another small rise with a much more defined overview. This gives you great views of the surrounding mountains, including the peak of Old Speck. You're getting closer, but you still have one final lunge ahead of you here. The hiking here is rocky and uneven, so take your time and step carefully.

At the 2-hour-and-40-minute mark, the trail splits. The A.T. and the Mahoosuc Trail head to the right. The trail to the summit heads to the left. At this point, you're just 0.3 mile from the summit of Old Speck. The final portion of the hike follows a much more moderate grade over a smoother trail surface. When you emerge from the dense mountaintop forest at the summit, you'll come to

**THE WATERFALLS PROVIDE BACKGROUND MUSIC DURING THE EARLY PART OF THE HIKE.**

a clearing and the fire tower. On a clear day, you feel as if you can see forever.

## Nearby Attractions

The rest of Grafton Notch State Park, the Sunday River resort area, and the town of Bethel, Maine, are nearby, all of which have numerous recreation, lodging, and dining options.

## Directions

From the intersection of US 2 and ME 26 just north of Sunday River in Newry, Maine, follow ME 26 about 12 miles north. The trailhead and parking area will be on the left (west) side of ME 26.

# **Baldpate Mountain**

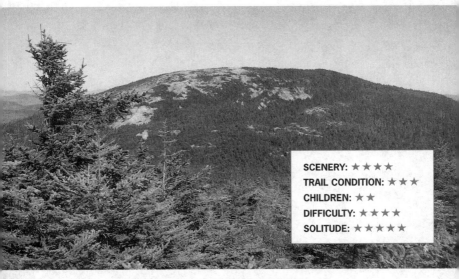

SCENERY: ★ ★ ★ ★
TRAIL CONDITION: ★ ★ ★
CHILDREN: ★ ★
DIFFICULTY: ★ ★ ★ ★
SOLITUDE: ★ ★ ★ ★ ★

**LOOKING OVER TO EAST PEAK OF BALDPATE MOUNTAIN**

**GPS TRAILHEAD COORDINATES:** N44° 35.416' W70° 56.783'

**DISTANCE & CONFIGURATION:** 5.8-mile out-and-back to West Peak; 7.6-mile out-and-back to East Peak

**HIKING TIME:** 4 hours to West Peak, 5.5 hours to East Peak

**HIGHLIGHTS:** Views of Mahoosuc Ridge from top, scenic hike on the way up

**ELEVATION:** West Peak: 3,680' at summit; East Peak: 3,812' at summit; 1,110' at trailhead

**ACCESS:** $3 parking fee at ME 26 parking area

**MAPS:** Appalachian Trail Conservancy *ME Map 7* and DeLorme *ME Atlas & Gazetteer Map 18*

**CONTACT:** Maine Department of Agriculture, Conservation and Forestry: **maine.gov/dacf**

## Overview

Baldpate Mountain is the true start of the Mahoosuc Range heading east, if you plan to make a longer trek. At the top, you'll be treated to sweeping views of the Mahoosuc Range to the north and east. It is a tough hike, though, especially the last hour.

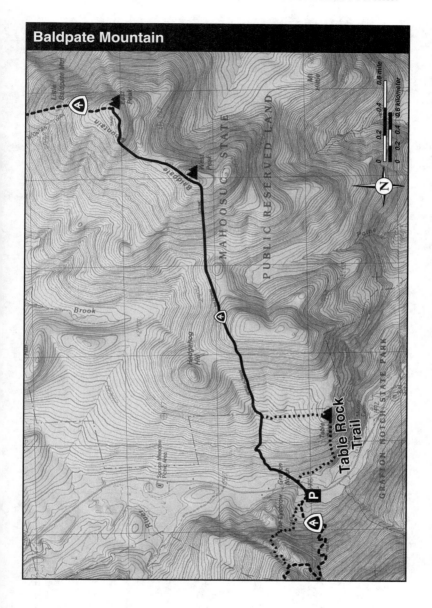

## Baldpate Mountain

## Route Details

For all the trailheads in this book that can be tough to find, you truly can't miss the trailhead for Baldpate Mountain. Carefully cross ME 26 from the parking area on the left (south–southwest) side of the road, and you'll see a huge wooden Appalachian Trail (A.T.) sign marking the trail's entrance. The path starts off flat and winds through a mixed forest of birch and conifers as it leads to the first intersection. You'll traverse a long series of A.T. footbridges before you get to the first intersection.

When you come to the wooden signpost, that's the point at which Table Rock Trail heads to the right. The A.T., heading to West Peak and East Peak of Baldpate, heads to the left. From here, it's 2.8 miles to West Peak. As soon as you bear off to the left, the trail begins to pitch upward, a portent of what is to come farther up the trail.

The surface here is quite firm, with roots and rocks making it a bit uneven. About 15 minutes into the hike, the trail veers to the right and gets steeper and more root covered. The sustained, steeper pitch continues. In the first steep pitch, the trail gets rockier and after about 20 minutes leads you up a fairly long stone staircase—the first of many. After that staircase, you'll pass some large boulders on the right, and the trail continues its steady, moderate climb.

Shortly after that, you'll come to a fairly good-size stream crossing. Several large boulders make it easy to hop over without getting your boots wet. At the 25-minute mark, the trail veers to the

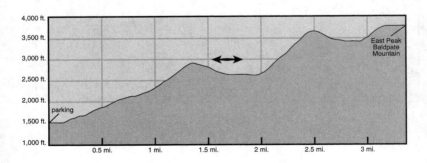

right at a wooden A.T. landmark sign. After that turn, it heads up straight for a sustained, steep to moderate climb over a rocky surface. The trail is wider here and certainly well-defined.

After that sustained climb, the trail becomes narrower again and the pitch relaxes slightly and only briefly. Then the trail again starts to get quite rocky, and you'll come to another signpost indicating a 0.5-mile spur trail off to the right to a view of Table Rock. You're at the 35-minute mark in the hike at this point. The view there is well worth the side trip if you have the energy and time.

Just after passing that sign and intersection, you'll cross another stream and continue on a rocky climb. The grade is consistent here, a steady, moderate climb that will indeed get your heart pumping. After about 45 minutes, the trail zigzags a bit and enters a grove of moderate-height birch and pine trees. The trail surface is almost like a natural root ladder here. Just past that, the trail continues snaking through the forest and travels up a steep stone staircase.

Now you're in a denser forest of conifers. The trail takes a sharp switchback to the right and continues to steadily climb over the uneven trail surface. There's another loose switchback to the left just after this. The trail here remains well-defined and well marked. That's the case with most of the trails in Grafton Notch State Park, as this is a popular hiking destination.

At the 1-hour mark, the trail actually flattens out for a while. This is a nice respite from an hour of steady, aggressive climbing. This nice rambling section follows around the mountain to the left (north). After about 10 minutes, the trail pitch again starts to pick up and starts rolling up and down. It's not the sustained climb that it was for the first hour. The trail continues rolling along as it heads over this plateau toward the first Baldpate peak.

In fact, you can start seeing the west peak of Baldpate towering overhead through the trees and you realize you still have a lot of mountain left ahead of you. After 1 hour and 30 minutes, you'll make another stream crossing, then the trail pitch again increases and the trail surface gets rockier. About 5 minutes later, you'll come to a short spur trail to the right that leads to the Baldpate lean-to.

After passing the lean-to, the trail pitch increases sharply and remains that way for most of the rest of the way. Now you're making the long, steep lunge to West Peak. This steep section has several switchbacks on its way to the peak. There are also several sections where you're hiking over open granite slab. These are often wet and can be slippery. The trail makes tighter switchbacks as you get higher on the mountain and closer to the peak. Then, after a seemingly relentless series of stone stairs and large granite slabs, you come out of the dense forest onto West Peak.

There's a sign indicating the true peak. Hike a bit farther and you'll find a couple of flat rocks upon which you can enjoy a break and the views of East Peak. From here, you can turn around; however, if you want to extend the hike, you can continue to East Peak. You could also do a point-to-point hike starting in Grafton Notch State Park and ending up farther east in the Mahoosuc Range. Whatever your intended destination, take a moment to enjoy the panoramic views of the Mahoosuc Range from atop Baldpate.

## Nearby Attractions

The rest of Grafton Notch State Park, the Sunday River resort area, and the town of Bethel, Maine, are nearby, all of which have numerous recreation, lodging, and dining options.

## Directions

From the intersection of US 2 and ME 26 just north of Sunday River in Newry, Maine, follow ME 26 about 12 miles north. The parking area will be on the left (west) side of ME 26. Cross over ME 26 to get to the Baldpate trailhead.

# Moody Mountain

**SCENERY:** ★ ★ ★ ★
**TRAIL CONDITION:** ★ ★ ★
**CHILDREN:** ★ ★ ★
**DIFFICULTY:** ★ ★ ★
**SOLITUDE:** ★ ★ ★ ★ ★

SOME PARTS OF THE APPALACHIAN TRAIL ARE WELL MARKED;
OTHERS NOT SO MUCH.

**GPS TRAILHEAD COORDINATES:** N44° 43.303' W70° 47.172'

**DISTANCE & CONFIGURATION:** 3-mile out-and-back

**HIKING TIME:** 1.75 hours

**HIGHLIGHTS:** Hike starts with stream crossing, sweeping views near top of Sawyer
Mountain to south

**ELEVATION:** 2,450' at summit, 1,080' at trailhead

**ACCESS:** Parking off South Arm Road where A.T. crosses road

**MAPS:** Appalachian Trail Conservancy *ME Map 7* and DeLorme *ME Atlas & Gazetteer Map 18*

**CONTACT:** Maine Appalachian Trail Club: **matc.org**

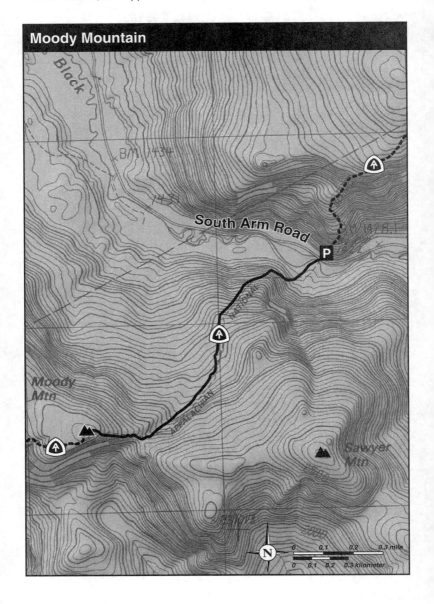

## Overview

Moody Mountain starts off with a steep, aggressive climb, but overall it's a nice ramble through the forest.

## Route Details

If you're walking around on South Arm Road looking for the Moody Mountain trailhead and can't seem to find it, keep looking. See that white blaze on the tree across the stream? Yep, that's it. The Moody Mountain Trail starts with an epic crossing of Black Brook. If the water is the least bit high, if there has been even a moderate amount of rain recently, you will get wet making this crossing. You are strongly advised to bring some water sandals. It might be low enough to hop from boulder to boulder, but then again it might be high enough to be knee-deep.

After crossing the stream, the trail starts out fairly narrow and firm but well-defined. Just a few minutes in, the trail pitch increases and you begin your ascent up Moody Mountain. As the trail gets steeper, the surface also gets rockier. The trail surface and pitch aren't too rugged, though.

After just 10 minutes, you'll cross an old dried-out streambed, then the trail begins a sustained, steeper, and circuitous ascent. While it does get slightly steep here, it's nothing compared to Old Blue Mountain across the street. Here the trail could benefit from

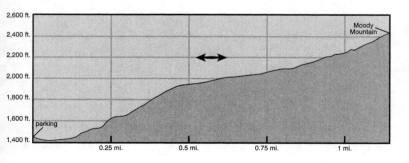

being better marked, so pay attention and keep an eye out for the white blazes.

The trail passes through a rock garden of large, moss-covered boulders at about the 15-minute mark, then climbs abruptly and veers to the left, making an almost 90-degree turn. After this, the trail maintains a steady, steeper climb over a rocky trail surface. You can definitely feel you're quickly gaining altitude in this stretch. Just look through the trees at the mountain across the street. Then the trail bears again to the left to follow the ridgeline away from the road in the southwesterly direction.

Then the trail switches back to the right and follows another steep, winding section. The footing can be treacherous here, so step carefully. A fall here would be costly, as the ground drops off dramatically to the right. Then the trail again seems to follow the ridgeline, and the pitch becomes more gradual. You're at about the 25-minute mark at this point.

A bit farther along the ridgeline, the trail pitch increases again. You're still on an extremely rocky surface as well. The sustained, steep trail takes you up another stone staircase. After the stone stairs, the trail pitch mellows slightly but only momentarily. Then the pitch picks right up again. The trail surface is still pretty rugged here with roots and rocks. It's also not all that well marked, so pay close attention. Many of the white blazes are fairly old and faded.

After about 35 minutes, the trail makes another dramatic 90-degree turn to the left, deeper into the backcountry. The trail is fairly well-defined here. At this point, you've reached another plateau, and the trail pitch relaxes for a while. After 40 minutes, you'll make another stream crossing, and then the trail takes you through a spectacular grove of maple trees. The trail is still making a sustained, moderate ascent, which is a nice break from the steep lunges earlier in the hike.

The loosely spaced forest of medium-height maples and ground cover of ferns provides for dramatic and brilliant colors, even when the sky is overcast. At the 50-minute mark, the trail surface again gets rockier and the trail pitch increases. The trail continues its sustained ascent. The trail is also better marked on this plateau. After 55 minutes of hiking, the trail heads to the right, up and out of a natural gorge between two peaks on either side.

This begins the short, steep, circuitous lunge to the summit of Moody Mountain. Closer to the top, the trail gets quite steep as it winds its way up toward the summit. On the way, there's one spot off to the left where you can catch a sweeping view of the mountains and hillsides to the southwest, including Sawyer Mountain. When you do reach the top, you'll find a giant pine tree providing good shade and a nice place to stop for a rest. The small summit cap of Moody Mountain is fairly densely forested, so there aren't many clear views from the top. That grand old pine tree is truly the defining feature.

## Nearby Attractions

Follow South Arm Road all the way to the end to reach the southern shores of Lower Richardson Lake.

## Directions

From US 2 in Hanover, Maine, follow ME 5 North 10.7 miles to ME 120 in Andover, and turn right. Follow ME 120 for 0.6 mile, and turn left onto South Arm Road. Follow South Arm Road 2.5 miles, veer left to stay on South Arm, and go another 5.1 miles to the trailhead crossing.

**39** # Old Blue Mountain

SCENERY: ★ ★ ★ ★ ★
TRAIL CONDITION: ★ ★ ★
CHILDREN: ★
DIFFICULTY: ★ ★ ★ ★ ★
SOLITUDE: ★ ★ ★ ★ ★

**ENJOY THIS VIEW FROM OLD BLUE MOUNTAIN TRAIL. YOU'VE EARNED IT.**

**GPS TRAILHEAD COORDINATES:** N44° 43.303' W70° 47.172'

**DISTANCE & CONFIGURATION:** 8.5-mile out-and-back

**HIKING TIME:** 5.5 hours

**HIGHLIGHTS:** Grueling initial climb, epic overlook with views of surrounding backcountry

**ELEVATION:** 3,642' at summit, 1,080' at trailhead

**ACCESS:** Parking on South Arm Road where A.T. crosses road

**MAPS:** Appalachian Trail Conservancy *ME Map 7* and DeLorme *ME Atlas & Gazetteer Map 18*

**CONTACT:** Maine Appalachian Trail Club: **matc.org**

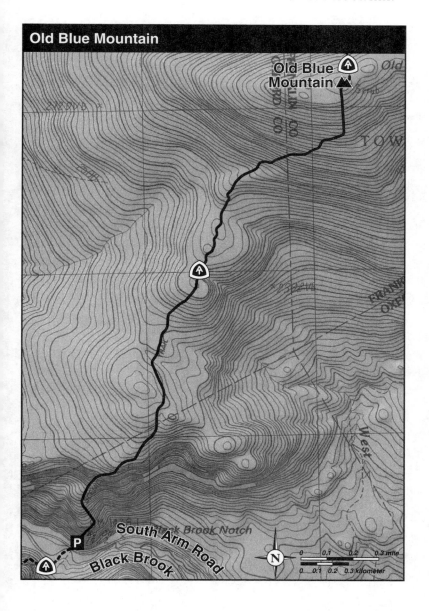

Old Blue Mountain

## Overview

The Old Blue Mountain hike starts off with a grueling climb up the side of the mountain, so be prepared. You'll be rewarded with some epic views.

## Route Details

The trailheads for Old Blue Mountain and Moody Mountain are on either side of South Arm Road. This long, winding road leads out of the town of Andover and into the unincorporated townships in northwestern Maine. The parcel of land is actually called North Andover Surplus. This is remote territory. Make sure your vehicle has a full tank of gas, there are no mechanical issues, and you have some food and water. It's not the end of the world, but if you do have any troubles out here, help will be a long time coming. And it is extremely unlikely that you will have a cell signal.

Hiking is not a particularly dangerous activity. It's worth noting, however, that the first hour of the Old Blue Mountain hike scrambles up the side of a steep, rocky cliff. This initial section of the Old Blue Mountain Trail is arguably the most dangerous hiking described in this book. A fall here would be extremely hazardous, as the cliff is steep and punctuated with trees and rocks. The trail's character, coupled with its remote location, is potentially hazardous. Be prepared and be careful.

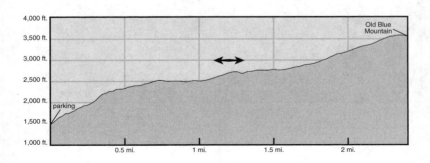

The Old Blue Mountain Trail starts off steep and rocky immediately as you enter the forest. Get used to it because it stays that way for a while. It goes from steep and rocky to extremely steep and rocky. Watch for the white blazes here because it would be fairly easy to wander off-trail, especially while focusing on the climbing at hand. About 50 feet into the hike, the trail veers right and continues its steep ascent.

This steep climb follows alongside a rocky ledge. The trail is fairly well-defined here, but it could probably benefit from a few more blazes so you know you're still on track. The steep and rocky climb up along the cliff continues. While the trail surface is extremely rocky, it provides good footsteps for climbing. Be extremely careful of your footing here. Take your time and watch your step. There are a few stone staircases in some of the steepest parts of the climb. After about 15 minutes of steep, rocky climbing, the trail winds to the left and up another steep stone staircase.

You're gaining altitude quite rapidly here. After another steep stone staircase, you'll come to a set of iron bars banged into the rock to help you get up and over. This section is brutal, but you'll soon be rewarded with views over to Moody Mountain and the backcountry to the north and west. After a couple more stone staircases, you'll come to part of the trail that's less rocky but no less steep. This leads to a longer, crescent-shaped stone staircase that leads around to the right. Here the trail is quite well-defined and also better marked than it is earlier in the hike.

The trail continues its relentless, steep, and rocky ascent. A mountain goat might even be complaining here. You'll come to a couple more stone staircases as you follow the steep trail up the side of the ridgeline. Again, the terrain here is demanding and dangerous. Take your time and watch your footing. A fall here would be disastrous.

After a couple of short switchbacks, you can start seeing more light coming through the surrounding forest. You have gained some serious altitude in short order here. Then you'll come to a section with dense undergrowth of short fir trees, even as the forest opens overhead. It's handy to have these trees to grab on to as you continue the steep climb. At about 45 minutes in at this point, you're faced with another section of steep hand-over-hand scrambling up rocks and roots. Be careful what you grab as handholds and use as footholds. Test them first before putting all your weight on them.

After about 50 minutes of brutally steep and rocky climbing and hand-over-hand scrambling, the trail actually starts to mellow out. You'll soon pass a small clearing on the right that rewards your effort with dramatic views of the backcountry and surrounding mountains and hillsides, as well as South Arm Road that led you out here.

After that scenic outlook, the trail pitches up again. Don't fall here either. The trail is a bit wider and safer to the left, but you don't even want to think about a tumble to the right. One hour into the hike, you'll come to another overlook. These views will energize you for the rest of the hike. Now the trail pitch is indeed more moderate, as you're following along the side of the ridgeline.

The trail rambles up through the woods then winds around to the right. The trail pitch definitely becomes more gradual for a longer section. Now it follows a moderate but steady ascent. As you ramble along the ridgeline, you'll pass through a dense undergrowth of ferns. This section is a nice break after the first hour of scrambling. As you continue in this second, more relaxing section of the trail, you'll come to a fascinating moss-covered rock garden at about 80 minutes into the hike.

Shortly after this, the trail pitch picks up again and the trail surface becomes much rockier. As you near the beginning of the final lunge to the summit, the trail takes a dramatic plunge down through a rock- and root-bound gully. Here you can catch glimpses of the summit through the trees. After crossing a stream at the bottom of this gully, you'll start climbing again.

The trail is fairly well marked here, as you hike over granite outcrops. You're about 2 hours into the hike now, and you can again see the summit looming ahead through the loosely spaced trees.

The trail is well-defined here. You pass through a narrow corridor of dense undergrowth over wet, angled granite slabs. Be careful here as well with your footing. The last 45 minutes of the hike is intensely rocky and slippery in spots. In some places, it feels like climbing up an active streambed.

As you emerge through the trees, you'll know you've come to the top. The summit is covered with short, scrubby conifers. There's a short side trail to the left (south) that leads to a small rock outcrop at the true summit. Stand here and drink in the view from the summit of Old Blue Mountain. You have truly earned it.

## Nearby Attractions

Follow South Arm Road all the way to the end to reach the southern shores of Lower Richardson Lake.

## Directions

From US 2 in Hanover, Maine, follow ME 5 North 10.7 miles to ME 120 in Andover, and turn right. Follow ME 120 for 0.6 mile, and turn left onto South Arm Road. Follow South Arm Road 2.5 miles, veer left to stay on South Arm, and go another 5.1 miles to the trailhead crossing.

SCENERY: ★ ★ ★ ★
TRAIL CONDITION: ★ ★ ★
CHILDREN: ★ ★ ★
DIFFICULTY: ★ ★ ★
SOLITUDE: ★ ★ ★ ★ ★

**THE BATES LEDGE TRAILHEAD IS CLEARLY MARKED.**

**GPS TRAILHEAD COORDINATES:** N44° 50.273' W70° 42.613'
**DISTANCE & CONFIGURATION:** 5.6-mile out-and-back
**HIKING TIME:** 4.25 hours
**HIGHLIGHTS:** Views of surrounding lakes and ponds nestled deep in the woods
**ELEVATION:** 2,700' at summit, 2,250' at trailhead
**ACCESS:** Parking on ME 17
**MAPS:** Appalachian Trail Conservancy *ME Map 6* and DeLorme *ME Atlas & Gazetteer Map 18*
**CONTACT:** Maine Appalachian Trail Club: **matc.org**

# Bates Ledge

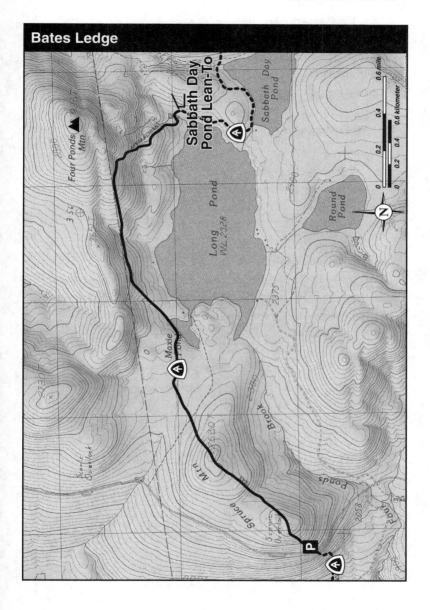

## Overview

Before you start, you'll have sweeping views of Mooselookmeguntic Lake to the west. Once in the woods, you'll hike into view of Moxie Pond and Long Pond.

## Route Details

Just the drive in to the trailhead is worth the effort for this hike. If you park in the scenic overlook area, you'll enjoy sweeping views of the lakes and mountains to the southwest. It is truly a spectacular view. The trailhead for Bates Ledge is across ME 17, heading northbound on the Appalachian Trail (A.T.). This section of the A.T. rises up and over Spruce Mountain at first, then up and along another ridgeline, then drops down again.

Once you climb the stone steps and enter the woods, the trail starts climbing right away. It's fairly well-defined here and has a surface of hard-packed dirt with rocks and roots. You're making a steady ascent through a mixed forest of mostly birch, maples, and pine.

About 5 minutes into the hike, the trail switches back to the left and continues its steady, moderate climb. The trail is a bit rockier and more root covered here, but it's also a bit less well-defined. Keep an eye on the white blazes to stay on the trail. Shortly after that, you'll come to a short, very steep, root- and rock-covered section.

The trail continues with a moderately steep, steady climb. You're getting quite a warm-up at this point. After about 10 minutes,

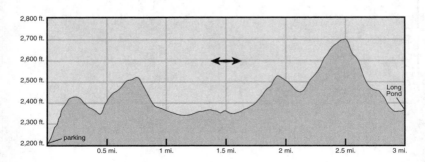

the trail pitch moderates somewhat, but the trail surface is still quite rugged with roots and rocks. There's a deep, lush green character to the forest here, as you're hiking through a dense undergrowth of ferns that blanket the forest floor.

Then about 15 minutes into the hike, you'll come to your first A.T. footbridge. After a fairly steep initial climb, the trail is more moderately pitched here. The trail rises and falls as it winds its way through the forest. This doesn't seem like a heavily used trail, save for the section hikers and thru-hikers who pass through here. About 20 minutes into the hike, the trail descends through a tiny clearing and field. It's really quite scenic and peaceful here. It could be very buggy in this section of the forest, though, so make sure you've got some bug repellent.

After that, the trail winds downhill through dense undergrowth on both sides. Then you'll come to another small clearing with a large grove of ferns. The initial scramble at the beginning of the hike was a quick warm-up. Now the trail is more of a gentle ramble along a ridgeline.

The trail is quite well-defined here, passing through dense undergrowth and a forest with a low, dense canopy. About 25 minutes into the hike, after a bit of gentle scrambling up and over some rocks, the trail abruptly begins a moderate steady climb. There are some loose rocks in this section, so watch your footing. After this and another relatively short, steep section, the trail pitch again becomes more moderate.

The trail surface is still quite uneven and rocky. You'll pass through a grove of densely packed, tight-needled conifers about 30 minutes into the hike. The trail is still taking you on a steady, moderate ascent. The trail remains well-defined here, though it's not all that well marked.

At about 50 minutes into the hike, the trail crosses another old fire road bed. There are a lot of these traversing the forests of New England. Follow the blazes and head straight across to stay on the A.T. Shortly after that crossing, you'll go over a series of A.T.

footbridges as you move through a boggy section. There's a short, rough, root- and rock-covered section, then another long series of A.T. footbridges.

Here you're hiking through a dramatic grove of tall, slender conifers. There's a dense, low undergrowth of ferns with the tall conifers overhead, which makes for quite a dramatically beautiful forest setting. You're about 1 hour into the hike at this point. The undergrowth becomes an increasingly tall blend of younger conifers, like a tree nursery at different stages of development.

After the tree nursery, the trail gets narrow and the surface gets rougher, with lots of roots and rocks and boggy sections. The pitch remains fairly moderate, though. At 1 hour and 15 minutes in, you'll pass Moxie Pond on the right. It would be tough to reach if you wanted to get in there and splash some water on your face, as it's surrounded by dense undergrowth. The trail surface is still quite rough here as well.

As the trail leads away from Moxie Pond, you'll pass through a loose birch grove as the trail heads toward the north. The trail is still narrow and rough but well-defined. Then, at about 1 hour and 35 minutes in, the trail begins a moderate and steady climb as you get closer to the apex of Bates Ledge. The trail rolls along, then crosses a stream and pitches up significantly over some rough root-bound and rock-covered sections. Then, after another steep pitch, you'll be able to see sweeping views of Long Pond to the right.

After catching a few views of the pond, the trail continues with moderate and steep sections, but with a sustained climb. After slightly less than 2 hours of hiking, you'll come to a massive rock ledge. The trail surface is still quite rough here as well. This is the beginning of the rock outcrops that make up Bates Ledge. The trail doesn't go all the way up and over the ledge, but there are plenty of rocks to rest on below the ledge.

After about 2 hours and 50 minutes of hiking, you've come to the highest point on the Bates Ledge Trail, with the massive rock of the ledge to your immediate left. This may be the high point on the trail, but if you continue and descend on the other side, you'll come to a couple of spots with a slightly more open view of Long Pond. You're at the 3-hour mark at this point. Another option is to continue up and over the ledge a bit farther on to the Sabbath Day Pond lean-to and use that as a turn-around spot.

Bates Ledge itself is a dramatic puzzle of sharp rocks and huge boulders. There's not a clearly defined, open summit, but there are dramatic views from the base of the ledge looking up and out toward Long Pond.

## Nearby Attractions

The lakes of western Maine, especially the Rangeley Lake and Saddle-back regions, are one of the primary outdoor recreation destinations in Maine, with opportunities for kayaking and canoeing, fishing, biking, more hiking, camping, and just relaxing.

## Directions

Follow ME 17 West out of Rumford, Maine. Go 24.7 miles, and park in the scenic overlook area off ME 17 overlooking Mooselookmegun-tic Lake or the dirt parking area about 0.5 mile down from the trail-head. From the scenic overlook, hike south on ME 17 to a break in the guardrail. Cross over here to the trailhead on the other side of the road. There's a white blaze on a significant set of stone steps leading up from the road.

# South Pond

**SCENERY:** ★ ★ ★ ★
**TRAIL CONDITION:** ★ ★ ★
**CHILDREN:** ★ ★ ★
**DIFFICULTY:** ★ ★ ★
**SOLITUDE:** ★ ★ ★ ★ ★

**SOUTH POND IS AS SCENIC AS IT IS REMOTE.**

**GPS TRAILHEAD COORDINATES:** N44° 53.213' W70° 32.447'

**DISTANCE & CONFIGURATION:** 4-mile out-and-back

**HIKING TIME:** 2.5 hours

**HIGHLIGHTS:** Spectacular and remote South Pond

**ELEVATION:** 2,150' at South Pond, 1,680' at trailhead

**ACCESS:** Parking area for trailhead on ME 4

**MAPS:** Appalachian Trail Conservancy *ME Map 6* and DeLorme *ME Atlas & Gazetteer Map 18*

**CONTACT:** Maine Appalachian Trail Club: **matc.org**

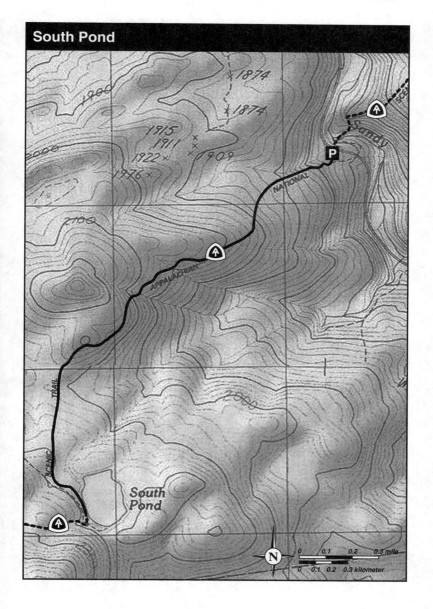

South Pond

## Overview

The hike out to South Pond meanders through the woods and offers some prime views of Saddleback Mountain and, of course, the pond itself.

## Route Details

The trail to South Pond starts off with a moderate rolling pitch. The trail surface is hard packed with lots of rocks poking through. Here you're hiking through a light forest of tall, slender maple and birch. Right off the bat, you'll come to a stream crossing, but it's an easy one to accomplish without getting your boots wet.

After that, the trail surface becomes a bit rougher, punctuated with roots and rocks. It's not all that well-defined here, or all that well marked, for that matter. So keep an eye out for the white blazes and be sure to pay attention. Then the trail pitches up to a slightly steeper yet still moderate grade and bears to the left.

Then you'll come to a short, steep section heavily covered with roots. It's like climbing a root staircase here. This can be really slick when it's wet, so watch your step. After another brief moderately steep section, the trail pitch mellows out again and continues on its way through the loosely spaced forest. Then you'll come to a tighter grove of young conifers.

The trail rolls up and down and winds through the woods. There are some spots where you have to step over large roots or rocks, but

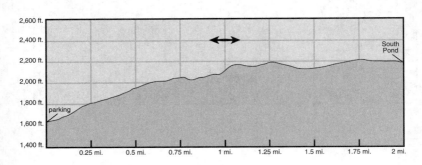

overall, it's a fairly mellow trail here. About 15 minutes into the hike, the undergrowth on either side of the trail becomes denser with lots of younger birch and pine. The surface here is still fairly rough with lots of roots and rocks.

The trail is climbing steadily here, but after a couple of short, steep pitches early on in the hike, it's mostly a moderate ramble. It's still punctuated with several flat sections and several short, steep sections. You're at about 30 minutes into the hike at this point, enjoying the path through the mixed forest.

At slightly more than 30 minutes into the hike, you'll pass through this truly scenic grove of tall, slender pines. The forest floor here is an undulating hillside with large rock ledges. The combination of the tall, slender pines and rock ledges gives this part of the forest a truly scenic, almost sculpted feel. If you could landscape the forest, this is how it would look. While the surrounding forest is indeed beautiful, the trail is only marginally well marked and well-defined here, so look down every now and then to ensure you're still on the trail.

The trail then winds through a large pile of moss-covered boulders on the right and continues to rise and fall through this spectacularly blissful section of the forest. The trail surface here is a soft cushion on pine needles, which feels great underfoot but can make staying on the actual trail a little more difficult. After passing through this pristine grove, the trail veers to the left and reenters the denser forest.

You're about 40 minutes into the hike now. The trail continues its steady yet moderate ascent. A bit farther in, you'll come to the base of a small hill. The trail gets significantly steeper here. You'll be stepping up and over roots and rocks and doing a bit of hand-over-hand scrambling. This steep section takes a sharp turn to the left, and then you're done. You're rewarded at the top with views of the mountains to the north through the loosely spaced trees. After that short, steep lunge, the trail continues its moderate climb through a forest of conifers.

The trail crests a rounded hilltop, then eases down on the far side. It's a nice, relaxed pace after that steep scramble. Over this hilltop, the trail takes you through a loosely spaced forest of short maple trees with dense undergrowth, so the trail is well-defined here. At about 1 hour into the hike, you're descending off this rounded hilltop. Toward the bottom, you'll come to a long series of Appalachian Trail (A.T.) footbridges.

After this section, the trail surface gets much rougher with roots and rocks but follows a fairly flat to moderate grade. The trail surface varies quite a bit in here between dense roots to swampy sections with A.T. footbridges. At about 1 hour and 30 minutes into the hike, you can start to see glimpses of South Pond through the trees to the left. You're almost there.

Shortly after, you'll come to an intersection where the A.T. bears to the right and a short spur trail leads down to the shore of South Pond. The water is delightfully clear and cool. There's a small encampment here, and it's a great place for a break or for lunch before heading back. While the trailhead is fairly remote and the trail surface is on the rough side, there isn't a ton of elevation gain with this one, so it would be good for slightly older kids with a good sense of adventure.

## Nearby Attractions

The lakes of western Maine, especially the Rangeley Lake and Saddleback regions, are one of the primary outdoor recreation destinations in Maine, with opportunities for kayaking and canoeing, fishing, biking, more hiking, camping, and just relaxing.

## Directions

From ME 27 north of Farmington, Maine, follow ME 4 North 8.5 miles, and then turn left to continue on ME 4 for another 19.4 miles, through Phillips and Madrid, Maine, to the parking area on the left (south) of ME 4.

# **West Carry Pond**

| | |
|---|---|
| **SCENERY:** ★ ★ ★ ★ |
| **TRAIL CONDITION:** ★ ★ ★ |
| **CHILDREN:** ★ ★ ★ |
| **DIFFICULTY:** ★ ★ ★ |
| **SOLITUDE:** ★ ★ ★ ★ ★ |

THE HIKE OUT TO WEST CARRY POND TAKES YOU DEEP INTO THE MAINE BACKCOUNTRY.

**GPS TRAILHEAD COORDINATES:** N45° 9.364' W70° 9.251'

**DISTANCE & CONFIGURATION:** 7.2-mile out-and-back

**HIKING TIME:** 3.5 hours

**HIGHLIGHTS:** Views of Saddleback and the pond itself

**ELEVATION:** 1,350' at West Carry Pond, 1,250' at trailhead

**ACCESS:** Parking alongside Long Falls Dam Road

**MAPS:** Appalachian Trail Conservancy *ME Map 5* and DeLorme *ME Atlas & Gazetteer Map 30*

**CONTACT:** Maine Appalachian Trail Club: **matc.org**

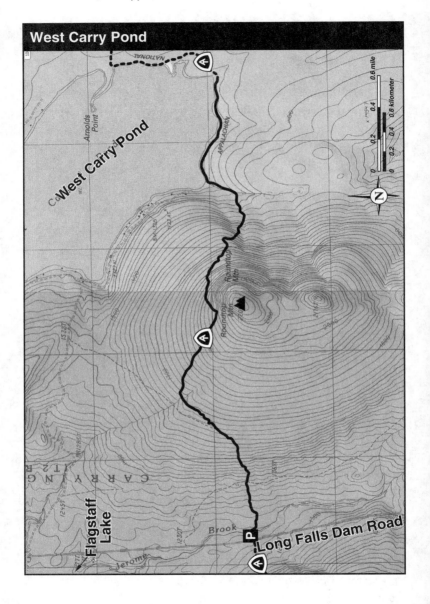

West Carry Pond

# Overview

This hike skirts up and around the side of Roundtop Mountain, then brings you to the shores of the remote and beautiful West Carry Pond.

# Route Details

The trail for Roundtop Mountain and West Carry Pond drops down off the Long Falls Dam Road and is immediately quite rough with lots of roots and rocks. Just 5 minutes into the hike, there's a major stream crossing. It's reasonable to make it across the stream by hopping from boulder to boulder, but if there has been a lot of rain recently, you might want to pack water sandals to make this crossing.

After you cross the stream, the path veers to the right. The trail surface here is quite rugged, with massive root networks cutting across the trail and lots of rocks but, thankfully, a moderate pitch. The narrow, twisting trail leads you through a grove of young conifers. The trail here is well-defined though extremely uneven and not all that well marked.

After about 15 minutes, the trail pitch picks up slightly to a moderate grade and follows through an open forest of conifers and birch. The trail surface also becomes much easier to navigate. The trail here is still meandering through a loose and breezy forest. After another small stream crossing, the pitch increases slightly and takes you through a beautiful birch grove.

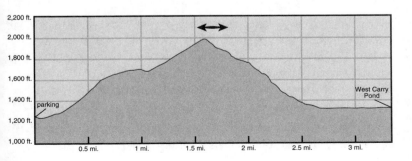

The trail is indeed better marked and defined here as the trail pitch begins a sustained yet moderate ascent. Unlike the first few moments of the hike, the trail surface is relatively smooth and dry. After about 20 minutes, the trail passes over on old fire road bed. Proceed straight across to continue on the Appalachian Trail (A.T.) southbound.

After you pass that old fire road, the trail pitches up slightly, but it's still not too steep. You're hiking through a shimmering birch forest of greens and golds. The trail is consistently steeper here as it zigs and zags through the forest. The trail is certainly well-defined here as it maintains a consistent climb through the mostly birch forest. There are more moderate sections, but you are steadily ascending.

After about 40 minutes of hiking, you'll notice that the trail becomes a bit wider, with a mellower grade. The character of the forest and the trail surface remains consistent, though. After that rugged initial section, the majority of this trail is a fairly relaxing ramble through the forest. At about the 50-minute mark, the trail reenters a more blended, dense forest of conifers and maples. Here the trail also becomes more narrow and rocky, all the while maintaining a consistent climb.

The trail is fairly well-defined here but could stand to be better marked. It continues its moderate ramble through the woods, skirting around the northwestern flank of the 2,240-foot Round Top Mountain. At this point, you're about 65 minutes into the hike. As you start getting closer to West Carry Pond, you're again hiking through a shimmering forest of mostly birch and maple.

After about 80 minutes of hiking and catching the first few glimpses of West Carry Pond through the trees to the left, you'll begin to descend steadily toward the pond. Shortly after that, you'll come to another stream crossing with an easy hop over a couple of boulders. Then the trail veers to the right and follows the course of the stream.

At the 1-hour-and-30-minute mark, as you're nearing West Carry Pond, the trail enters a majestic grove of tall conifers. There's a dense undergrowth of baby conifers covering the forest floor. The trail surface here is quite rugged, with lots of roots and rocks. It's not all that well-defined either, so keep an eye on the white blazes. Here you're starting to see closer views of the pond through the woods to the left. Soon the trail will follow along the shores of West Carry Pond.

The dense forest extends right the shoreline, so continue to the West Carry Pond lean-to, which is off in the woods on the other side of the trail. Close to where the short trail leads off to the lean-to, there's a small clearing at the shore of the pond. This is a perfect spot to relax and enjoy the pristine beauty of West Carry Pond.

## Nearby Attractions

Long Falls Dam Road follows the eastern side of Flagstaff Lake, which is a popular recreation destination.

## Directions

From ME 27 in Kingfield, Maine, follow ME 16 East 7.5 miles. Turn left onto Long Falls Dam Road, and in 0.4 mile, veer left to stay on Long Falls Dam Road. Follow the road for 19 miles to where the A.T. crosses the road. It can be difficult to spot. There are orange tags on the telephone poles. The trailhead is just past the pole marked 390. If you pass Boise Road on the right, you've missed it by about 0.5 mile. Turn around and continue slowly. You'll see a trailhead for the Maine Hut Trails, then the A.T. crossing shortly thereafter.

The West Carry Pond trailhead will be on the right (east) as you're heading north on Long Falls Dam Road, or on the left if you missed it and are driving back. You'll see a large boulder with a white blaze on the opposite side of the road. Pull off the road and park along the roadside.

**43** # Pleasant Pond Mountain

THE PLEASANT POND MOUNTAIN HIKE WILL TEST YOUR METTLE.

SCENERY: ★ ★ ★ ★ ★
TRAIL CONDITION: ★ ★ ★
CHILDREN: ★ ★ ★
DIFFICULTY: ★ ★ ★
SOLITUDE: ★ ★ ★ ★ ★

**GPS TRAILHEAD COORDINATES:** N45° 16.376' W69° 55.323'

**DISTANCE & CONFIGURATION:** 2.8-mile out-and-back

**HIKING TIME:** 2.5 hours

**HIGHLIGHTS:** Panoramic views from summit

**ELEVATION:** 2,477' at summit, 1,240' at trailhead

**ACCESS:** Small parking off of Hangtown Road

**MAPS:** Appalachian Trail Conservancy *ME Map 4* and DeLorme *ME Atlas & Gazetteer Map 30*

**CONTACT:** Maine Appalachian Trail Club: **matc.org**

# Pleasant Pond Mountain

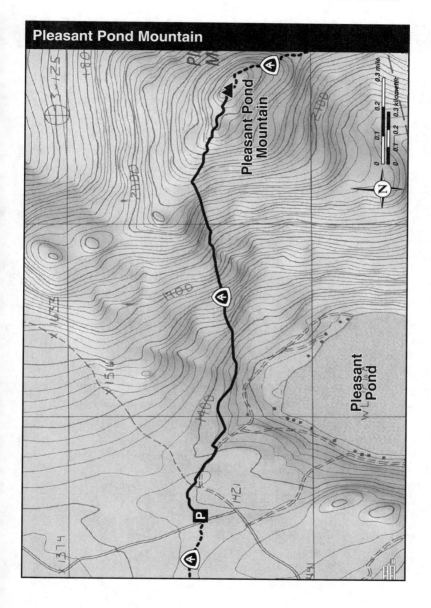

## Overview

This short but impressively steep and rocky trail brings you to an open granite cap with sweeping views of the surrounding backcountry.

## Route Details

The trailhead for Pleasant Pond Mountain is quite remote. Just about 0.5 mile after Hangtown Road turns into a dirt road, you'll turn off to the right to a small parking area marked by a very small sign directing you to the trailhead and trailhead parking. Pay close attention, as it's easy to miss.

At the trailhead, you'll see a sign indicating it's 1.4 miles to the summit of Pleasant Pond Mountain. The trail starts off flat, wide, and well-defined, over a hard-packed surface with just a few roots poking through. Follow this wide section of trail for about 8–10 minutes, when the wide trail (possibly a snowmobile trail) heads straight and the Appalachian Trail (A.T.) veers to the left into the dense forest of maple, birch, and conifers.

Now the trail is much narrower and winding. As soon as the A.T. heads into the woods, you'll go over a small stream crossing. The trail surface here is extremely rocky and root-bound. It's twisty and winding but well marked and fairly well-defined. At this early stage of the hike, the trail is rolling up and down through the woods at a fairly moderate grade.

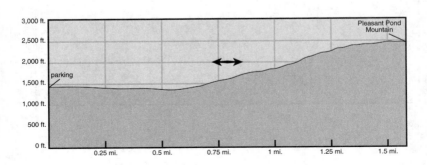

In spots, the trail is so rocky it almost feels like hiking up an old streambed. The roots can also be quite slippery, so watch your footing. After about 15 minutes, you'll pass over a few old A.T. footbridges to get you over a swampy section of the trail. You'll traverse a few more just moments later. The trail surface here is still quite rugged, though the grade is moderate. Shortly thereafter, you'll pass over another stream crossing.

At 0.3 mile into the hike, you'll come to an intersection with a short spur trail down to the shores of Pleasant Pond. This would be a nice break on a hot summer day. Shortly after that intersection, you'll come to a stone staircase. After that, the trail gets much steeper and for the most part stays that way. The trail surface also maintains its rugged, rocky character.

After about 25 minutes of hiking, you'll come to another stream crossing that would be a good place to get water. As always, you should treat or filter any water you procure in the wild. After that stream crossing, the rocky trail starts getting steep and switches back and forth up the mountainside. The trail is a bit less well-defined here in this tight series of switchbacks, so be sure to pay attention to the blazes and where the trail is taking you.

Overall, the Pleasant Pond Mountain Trail may not be that long, but it is impressively steep. It's like a root-and-rock jungle gym. There are also many spots, like at about 30 minutes into the hike, where it's not all that well-defined or well marked. You'll always be happy to see a white blaze to assure you you're still on the trail in those sections.

The steep, rocky trail continues its steady, circuitous climb. You'll ascend another stone staircase as you continue up. The steep grade is relentless in this section about 40 minutes into the hike. You'll climb up stone staircases and huge granite outcrops crossed with large roots. Be sure to watch your step and take your time. After passing through an open section with some hand-over-hand climbing up rock outcrops, the trail reenters the dense forest.

**THE GRANITE SUMMIT CAP OF PLEASANT POND MOUNTAIN OPENS
TO SWEEPING VIEWS.**

Here the trail is much narrower as it passes into a low, dense grove of conifers. It's much better defined here, what with the dense forest on both sides. The sustained, steep climb continues, moving up a natural staircase of large rocks and root networks. The trail here is steep, narrow, and circuitous, but at least it is back to being fairly well-defined, so it's easy to follow.

After about 50 minutes of hiking, you'll make a big switchback to the left and start to see nice views of Pleasant Pond through the forest below you. Now you're hiking along a ridgeline over a fairly muddy surface. The trail follows a steep side hill and the surface is muddy, so the footing can be treacherous here.

A bit farther along and the trail will make another dramatic switchback, this time to the right. The trail surface is still muddy and loose, so step slowly and deliberately. The trail maintains its steady ascent, and slowly the trail surface gets a bit more firm and dry.

Here, nearing the summit plateau, the ground cover is a dense grove of young conifers, which lends a verdant character to the forest. The trail is well-defined in here and fairly well marked. Just past this grove of young conifers, the trail veers slightly left and passes over an extremely treacherous section of roots and rocks. Take your time and step carefully. You're just below the top at this point.

At about 70 minutes into the hike, you'll come to a large rock ledge to scramble up and over. This is the beginning of the massive granite summit cap. The dense forest of short conifers encircling the summit cap is a bit too dense for a view of Pleasant Pond, but there are commanding views of the backcountry to the west and north.

Traverse the rock ledge at the summit and follow the trail back into the woods. Then a few moments later, you'll come out onto another open granite cap that is truly the summit. The view is a bit better from the granite outcrop just below the summit.

## Nearby Attractions

This trailhead is near the headquarters and campground for Northern Outdoors, a renowned whitewater rafting company that runs trips on the Kennebec, Penobscot, and Dead Rivers.

## Directions

Follow US 201 to the town of Caratunk, Maine. Bear right onto Hangtown Road, and go about 4 miles. About 0.5 mile after Hangtown Road turns to dirt, there will be a small parking area off to the right marked by a very small sign. Go slow and be careful, as it's easy to miss.

# Little and Big Niagara Falls

SCENERY: ★ ★ ★ ★
TRAIL CONDITION: ★ ★ ★ ★
CHILDREN: ★ ★ ★ ★
DIFFICULTY: ★ ★
SOLITUDE: ★ ★ ★ ★

**LITTLE AND BIG NIAGARA FALLS ARE SOME OF THE MOST IMPRESSIVE WATERFALLS ON THE APPALACHIAN TRAIL IN NEW ENGLAND.**

**GPS TRAILHEAD COORDINATES:** N45° 53.133' W69° 0.015'

**DISTANCE & CONFIGURATION:** 6.2-mile out-and-back

**HIKING TIME:** 4.25 hours

**HIGHLIGHTS:** Spectacular views of both waterfalls

**ELEVATION:** 800' at Big Niagara Falls; 1,100' at Little Niagara Falls; 1,100' at trailhead

**ACCESS:** Enter through Baxter State Park Togue Pond Gate ($14 cash access fee; road closed in winter)

**MAPS:** Appalachian Trail Conservancy *ME Map 1*, DeLorme *ME Atlas & Gazetteer Map 50*, and Baxter State Park *Katahdin Lake Trailhead* map

**CONTACT:** Baxter State Park: **baxterstateparkauthority.com**

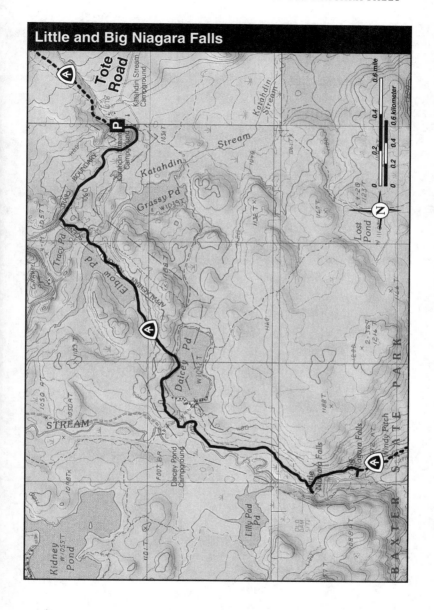

Little and Big Niagara Falls

## Overview

This is a fantastic, kid-friendly hike to dramatic waterfalls as the Nesowadnehunk Brook cascades over the rocks.

## Route Details

Katahdin is clearly the star of Baxter State Park, but it's by no means the only peak or excellent hiking route. Head southbound on the Appalachian Trail (A.T.) out of Katahdin Stream Campground and you'll find Little and Big Niagara Falls. The trailhead for Little and Big Niagara Falls is just across the Park Tote Road from the Katahdin Stream Campground. You start off on a nice hard-packed surface following a gentle rolling grade on a well-defined and well-marked trail. This is a great option for the day after Katahdin, or even two days after, as it's a fairly relaxing ramble through the dense forest of birch, maple, and conifers.

At just 10 minutes into the hike, you'll come to an A.T. footbridge crossing a stream. The trail starts gently rolling up and down and the trail surface gets more root covered. The well-defined trail passes through the lush green undergrowth blanketing the forest floor. Whereas the Hunt Trail and other routes up Katahdin are quite popular, you're likely to have this section of the trail to yourself.

The trail still follows a relatively flat, rolling, gentle ramble through the forest. At 15 minutes into the hike, there's an almost

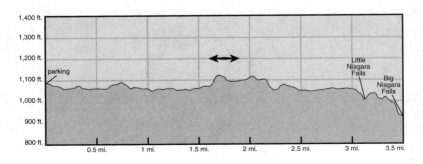

junglelike quality to the forest with the moss-covered rocks and tree stumps. The trail starts to rise and fall a bit more as you get farther along. Here the forest is mostly tall, slender pines.

A bit farther along, at about 25 minutes into the hike, you'll cross a series of A.T. footbridges—some single and some double width. These can be slippery on wet days, so be sure to watch your step. These footbridges bring you across a mossy grove and then another stream crossing. There's another long series of footbridges after the stream crossing to get you through this boggy area.

After the long series of footbridges, the trail continues its gentle ramble. You can start to see Grassy Pond through the forest to the right. After the first few glimpses of Grassy Pond, the trail passes through a dense corridor of tightly packed conifers. The air is heavy with the scent of conifers. This lush green corridor of conifers continues around a corner in view of Grassy Pond.

Once you've passed through that tight row of pines, you'll come to another series of A.T. footbridges at about 45 minutes into the hike. Now the surrounding pine forest is slightly taller and older. The trail surface is still a relatively smooth cover of pine needles with a few roots poking up. The forest here is truly spectacular, with a dense cover of moss, an undergrowth of young conifers, and a forest canopy composed of tall, stately pines. Here you'll pass the intersection to the Grassy Pond Trail to the right. Follow the A.T. toward Daicey Pond to the left.

The trail continues to rise and fall, but there's no appreciable elevation gain or loss here. The forest still has a lush, junglelike character. After a bit more than 1 hour of hiking, you'll start to see Daicey Pond through the forest ahead. The A.T. leads right to Daicey Pond and follows around the border to the right (west). Here, in view of Daicey Pond, the trail surface is quite rough with roots and rocks. One hour and 15 minutes into the hike, there's another intersection with a trail off to the right and the A.T. continues straight (south).

As you loop around Daicey Pond, you'll see the Daicey Pond campsites on the other side. The trail southbound is well-defined as it passes through dense undergrowth. You leave the side of Daicey Pond and the trail rolls up and down through the increasingly dense forest. One hour and 30 minutes into the hike, you'll pass through the parking area for Daicey Pond. Proceed straight across to continue on the A.T. This would be a good alternate starting spot if you're camping at Daicey Pond or if you wanted to drive here with smaller kids—or even adults who may be sore from Katahdin. You're about 30 minutes from the falls at this point.

The rest of the trail leading to Little and Big Niagara Falls is similar in character. You'll pass over another set of A.T. footbridges, then proceed on the root- and rock-covered trail. As the trail descends down a slight grade and bears to the left, it will follow the path of Katahdin Stream. Here the trail is quite wide and flat—perfect for smaller kids.

The falls are 1.2 miles from the Daicey Pond parking area. You're about 2 hours into the hike at this point, and you can start to hear the rush of water of the falls. You'll come to where the trail splits to Little Niagara Falls. The falls are 150 feet from the intersection. By all means, head down there and enjoy the falls, but don't forget to continue to Big Niagara Falls.

Big Niagara Falls are 0.3 mile farther down the A.T. southbound, which is only about 15 minutes. Big Niagara Falls are indeed impressive. You can hike down to and out on the rocks, but do be extremely careful. There's a lot of water rushing through there, and you do not want to fall. That said, there are plenty of places to just sit and relax and enjoy the dramatic falls.

## Nearby Attractions

All of Baxter State Park is an epic destination for hiking, canoeing, and climbing. Plan to spend some additional time camping at any of Baxter's campgrounds and remote campsites.

**THE HIKE SOUTH TO THE FALLS FOLLOWS A WELL-DEFINED TRAIL.**

## Directions

From I-95, take Exit 244. Turn left onto ME 157 West, and go 11.3 miles to Millinocket, Maine (an officially designated Appalachian Trail Community). Turn right onto Katahdin Avenue, take an immediate left onto Bates Street (which turns into Millinocket Road), and go 8.2 miles. Continue on Baxter State Park Road, entering through the Togue Pond Gatehouse, and go a total of 8.7 miles on this road. Turn left onto Park Tote Road, and go 7.8 miles to Katahdin Stream Campground.

**Katahdin**

SCENERY: ★ ★ ★ ★ ★
TRAIL CONDITION: ★ ★ ★
CHILDREN: ★
DIFFICULTY: ★ ★ ★ ★ ★
SOLITUDE: ★ ★ ★

**THE HUNT SPUR ON THE WESTERN FLANK OF THE MIGHTY KATAHDIN IS NOT FOR THE FAINTHEARTED.**

**GPS TRAILHEAD COORDINATES:** N45° 53.133' W69° 0.015'

**DISTANCE & CONFIGURATION:** 10.4-mile out-and-back

**HIKING TIME:** 8–10 hours

**HIGHLIGHTS:** Epic climb, scrambling over Hunt Spur, views from the summit

**ELEVATION:** 5,268' at summit, 1,100' at trailhead

**ACCESS:** Enter through Baxter State Park Togue Pond Gate ($14 cash access fee; road closed in winter)

**MAPS:** Appalachian Trail Conservancy *ME Map 1*, DeLorme *ME Atlas & Gazetteer Map 50*, and Baxter State Park *Katahdin Lake Trailhead* map

**CONTACT:** Baxter State Park: **baxterstateparkauthority.com**

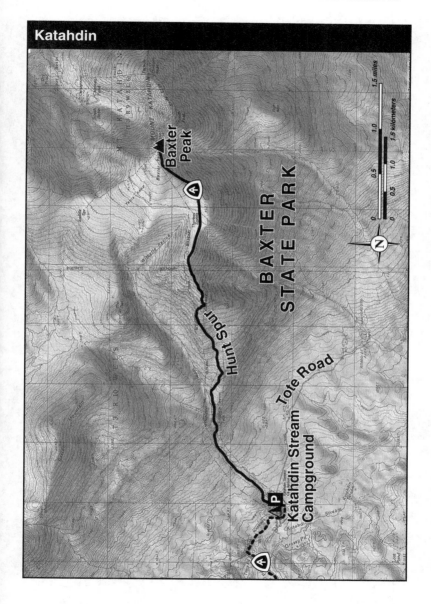

## Overview

This is the big one—the longest, most difficult hike presented in this book. It's also the northern terminus of the Appalachian Trail (A.T.). Be prepared for a true backcountry adventure that is well worth the effort.

## Route Details

The trailhead for the Hunt Spur Trail—also the final northbound section of the A.T.— runs out of the northeastern side of the Katahdin Stream Campground. This is the place from which to launch your Katahdin adventure. This is an extremely long and strenuous hike. There is no easy route up to the summit of Katahdin. Be prepared, be well rested, and start early.

You could do Katahdin as a day trip, but why torture yourself? That would be an extremely long day. The average round-trip hike time is 8–10 hours. Treat yourself and camp at Katahdin Stream the night before and after.

It's also advisable to buy one of the official hiking route maps at the visitor center. These waterproof maps have all the hiking routes and distances and other information. The 5.2-mile route to the summit is broken up as follows: 1.1 miles to the Owl Trail split, then 3.1 miles up and over the Hunt Spur, then the final 1.1 miles to the summit from the top of the Hunt Spur. The first and last miles are relatively easy, but those 3.1 miles in the middle are extremely strenuous and treacherous.

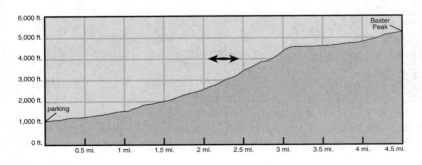

The Hunt Trail is a popular hiking route. On a nice day, you can expect quite a bit of company. There will be a conga line of people heading up the trail. The first section of the trail starts off relatively mellow, following the path of Katahdin Stream. It quickly starts becoming rockier and more root-bound. The forest is a dense mix of birch and various conifers. About 15 minutes into the hike, there's a nice overlook to Katahdin Stream.

After that, the trail starts getting rockier and continues its steady, moderate ascent as it snakes back and forth through the forest. At about 35 minutes in, you'll pass through a rock garden of huge boulders. Then a bit farther down the trail, you'll come to the intersection with the Owl Trail at 1.1 miles. Just after this, you'll pass over Katahdin Stream on a major footbridge. The view of Katahdin Stream Falls here is spectacular. Take a moment to relax here, as the real climbing is about to begin in earnest. On the other side of the Katahdin Stream Falls bridge, there's an outhouse if you're in the mood.

After crossing the bridge, the trail veers to the left and follows a steep, open outcrop of granite. After ascending this, you'll come to another large granite ledge. At the top of this ledge, you'll get your first of many open views of the surrounding backcountry to the west. After this, the trail pitches steeply upward and the trail surface becomes much rockier. Several long, stone staircases here help ease the ascent.

After several stone staircases, the trail gets much narrower and rockier. It's quite well-defined as it winds through dense undergrowth. The trail pitch mellows slightly for a moment here but continues its steady ascent. At about 1 hour and 15 minutes into the hike here, the trail again picks up a steep, sustained pitch. The trail is still quite rocky here. You definitely have the feeling of having gained some altitude already, but you still have a ways to go yet.

At the 2-hour mark, there's a short stream crossing and the trail cuts through a dense grove of pines. Take a moment to breathe in that rich, heady balsam scent. After this grove, the trail gets quite narrow and maintains its steep, rocky, sustained ascent.

After this, the Hunt Spur Trail just continues to grow rockier, steeper, and more treacherous. Be extremely careful here and take your time. The surrounding forest gets shorter up here as well, another sign that you're gaining some elevation. The trail takes a series of tight switchbacks, so keep an eye on the white blazes to ensure you stay on the trail. At slightly more than 2 hours into the hike, you begin some hand-over-hand scrambling over the large boulders and rock gardens that make up the trail. This is even before you are truly on the Hunt Spur. It is strenuous climbing, so again—exercise caution and take your time.

After about 3 hours, you are truly on the Hunt Spur. This is almost 1 hour of challenging hand-over-hand scrambling and navigating your way through the puzzle of huge boulders and passageways. Be extra careful to follow the white blazes here. You would not want to wander too far off-trail here. The Hunt Spur is not hiking; it is nontechnical rock climbing.

In a couple of spots where you would need a rope or other climbing gear to successfully make a traverse or ascent, you'll find iron bars hammered into the rock. The Hunt Spur takes more than 1 hour to navigate. It is extremely steep in spots. Just when you feel as if you'll never crest this rock maze, you come over the top of the Hunt Spur.

Now you're facing the Tablelands and 1.1 more miles to the summit, which you can see ahead of you when it's not too cloudy. The trail up and over the Tablelands is relatively mellow compared to the Hunt Spur, but it's still quite rocky. There are also zones of delicate alpine vegetation and trail restoration efforts, so make sure you stay on the trail here.

The trail grows rockier as you approach the final push to the summit. When you see the faded and worn wooden sawhorse that marks the summit of Katahdin, congratulate yourself. You stand atop the highest peak in the state of Maine and the northern terminus of the Appalachian Trail. The views from the summit of Katahdin are outstanding. You can see the backcountry of Maine in 360 degrees.

As you make your plans to ascend Katahdin, be sure to save energy, water, and supplies for the trip down. Descending the Hunt Spur can be as challenging as the way up. Again, be particularly cautious to follow the white blazes. This is probably some of the most difficult hiking you're likely to encounter in New England. Katahdin—and indeed the rest of Baxter State Park, as well as the forests, mountains, and lakes surrounding it for as far as the eye can see—is true remote northern backcountry.

## Nearby Attractions

All of Baxter State Park is an epic destination for hiking, canoeing, and climbing. Plan to spend some additional time camping at any of Baxter's campgrounds and remote campsites.

## Directions

From I-95, take Exit 244. Turn left onto ME 157 West, and go 11.3 miles to Millinocket, Maine (an officially designated Appalachian Trail Community). Turn right onto Katahdin Avenue, take an immediate left onto Bates Street (which turns into Millinocket Road), and go 8.2 miles. Continue on Baxter State Park Road, entering through the Togue Pond Gatehouse, and go a total of 8.7 miles on this road. Turn left onto Park Tote Road, and go 7.8 miles to Katahdin Stream Campground.

# Appendixes & Index

**THE ROCKY TRAIL TO THE SUMMIT OF KATAHDIN IS A TRUE TEST OF LEGS AND SPIRIT.** *(See page 264.)*

**OPPOSITE: THE OBSERVATION TOWER ATOP OLD SPECK OFFERS A VIEW OF THE ENTIRE MAHOOSUC RANGE IN WESTERN MAINE.** *(See page 214.)*

# Appendix A:

## Contact Information

### CONNECTICUT

**CONNECTICUT DEPARTMENT OF ENERGY AND ENVIRONMENTAL PROTECTION**
860-424-3000
ct.gov/deep

### MASSACHUSETTS

**MASSACHUSETTS EXECUTIVE OFFICE OF ENERGY AND ENVIRONMENTAL AFFAIRS**
617-626-1000
mass.gov/eea

**MASSACHUSETTS DEPARTMENT OF CONSERVATION AND RECREATION**
617-626-1250
mass.gov/eea/agencies/dcr

### VERMONT

**VERMONT STATE PARKS**
888-409-7579
vtstateparks.com

**GREEN MOUNTAIN NATIONAL FOREST**
802-747-6700
www.fs.usda.gov/fingerlakes

### NEW HAMPSHIRE

**NEW HAMPSHIRE DIVISION OF PARKS AND RECREATION**
603-271-3556
nhstateparks.com

**WHITE MOUNTAIN NATIONAL FOREST**
603-536-6100
www.fs.usda.gov/whitemountain

### MAINE

**MAINE BUREAU OF PARKS AND LANDS**
207-287-3821
maine.gov/dacf/parks

**BAXTER STATE PARK**
207-723-5140
baxterstateparkauthority.com

# Appendix B:
## Appalachian Trail Communities

The Appalachian Trail Community program is an Appalachian Trail Conservancy initiative that seeks to develop mutually beneficial relationships with interested towns and counties along the Appalachian Trail to enhance their economies, further protect the trail, and engage a new generation of volunteers.

**MASSACHUSETTS**
Great Barrington

**NEW HAMPSHIRE**
Hanover

**VERMONT**
Norwich

**MAINE**
Millinocket
Monson
Rangeley

# Index

# About the Author

**LAFE LOW, A LIFELONG NEW ENGLANDER,** spends nearly all of his free time outside—skiing, hiking, skiing, camping, skiing, kayaking, skiing . . . you get the picture. He has nearly reached his goal of having his garage look like an Eastern Mountain Sports or REI store.

After earning a bachelor of arts degree in journalism from Keene State College in 1984, Lafe went to work in the magazine world. After working for a variety of technology publications, he launched his own magazine, *Explore New England,* in 1995. This was truly the crossroads of his personal and professional passions. After *Explore New England,* he went on to be the editor of *Outdoor Adven-*

*Photographed by Peter Tamposi*

*ture* and an editor with Globe Pequot Press. While he is now back in the technology world, he still writes about the outdoors to feed his passion. His first book, *Best Tent Camping: New England,* was first published in 2002. The fourth edition was published in 2012. *Best Hikes of the Appalachian Trail: New England* is his second book, and certainly not his last. He lives in the Boston area.

# About the Appalachian Trail Conservancy

**THE APPALACHIAN TRAIL** (A.T.) is incredibly well-known around the world, not just among the diverse hiking and backpacking communities. Less well-known is what put it on the ground in the 1920s and '30s and manages it to this day: the staff and more than 6,000 volunteers under the umbrella of the Appalachian Trail Conservancy, founded in 1925 by 22 pioneers.

Yes, the A.T. has been a part of the national park system since 1968, but part of the deal with Congress was that this small, private, nonprofit organization would continue to do the bulk of the work and raise most of the money to pay for that work—rather than have taxpayers underwrite what would be a typical national park staff to care for 250,000 acres of public land. (The National Park Service does have a small A.T. office of fewer than a dozen employees working with us on major legal issues of environmental and historic preservation compliance and law enforcement.)

What does "take care of" mean? It means keeping the footpath of more than 2,189 miles open and safe for outdoor recreation of most nonmotorized types (including hunting for about half the area). It means maintaining in good condition overnight shelters and tent sites, absolutely necessary bridges, and other facilities.

It means monitoring the health of more than 550 rare, threatened, or endangered species that call the trail lands home (we don't yet have a count on the animals)—more than almost any other national park. It means preserving more cultural artifacts still in place than in any other park. (Remember, these ridgelines were the Colonial frontier before the seas and the West, and they were the site of Underground Railroad stops and then dozens of Civil War battles, as well as farms taken over by freed slaves.)

It means working cooperatively with the National Park Service, U.S. Forest Service, and 14 states that hold title to those lands for the public—altogether almost 100 agency partners. It means bringing into the fold for mutual benefit 85 counties' officials and the governments and businesses for almost three dozen places officially designated as an Appalachian Trail Community. It means watching for and combating threats to all from incompatible development.

It means providing the public with timely, comprehensive, and useful information about the A.T.'s wealth of natural beauty and how best to enjoy it—for example, through books such as this, in which we are proud to have a role.

We consider it our job to conserve, promote, and enhance the Appalachian National Scenic Trail every day. We do all that for less than $6.75 in private funds per day per mile (and about $2.75 more in targeted federal contracts).

You can support that effort by going to **appalachiantrail.org** to learn more and/or become a member. Old school (like us)? You can write to Appalachian Trail Conservancy, P.O. Box 807, Harpers Ferry, WV 25425, or call 304-535-6331.

Most of all, we hope that you enjoy in some way the People's Path. It *is* yours, after all.

**DEAR CUSTOMERS AND FRIENDS,**

**SUPPORTING YOUR INTEREST IN OUTDOOR ADVENTURE,** travel, and an active lifestyle is central to our operations, from the authors we choose to the locations we detail to the way we design our books. Menasha Ridge Press was incorporated in 1982 by a group of veteran outdoorsmen and professional outfitters. For many years now, we've specialized in creating books that benefit the outdoors enthusiast.

Almost immediately, Menasha Ridge Press earned a reputation for revolutionizing outdoors- and travel-guidebook publishing. For such activities as canoeing, kayaking, hiking, backpacking, and mountain biking, we established new standards of quality that transformed the whole genre, resulting in outdoor-recreation guides of great sophistication and solid content. Menasha Ridge continues to be outdoor publishing's greatest innovator.

The folks at Menasha Ridge Press are as at home on a white-water river or mountain trail as they are editing a manuscript. The books we build for you are the best they can be, because we're responding to your needs. Plus, we use and depend on them ourselves.

We look forward to seeing you on the river or the trail. If you'd like to contact us directly, join in at www.trekalong.com or visit us at www.menasharidge.com. We thank you for your interest in our books and the natural world around us all.

**SAFE TRAVELS,**

**BOB SEHLINGER**
**PUBLISHER**